find the JOYFUL LEADER within

BANISHING BURNOUT IN EARLY CHILDHOOD EDUCATION

TERESA A. BYINGTON, PHD

Gryphon House
www.gryphonhouse.com

Published by Gryphon House, Inc.
P. O. Box 10, Lewisville, NC 27023
800.638.0928; 877.638.7576 [fax]
Visit us on the web at www.gryphonhouse.com.

Library of Congress Control Number: 2023931230

Bulk Purchase

Gryphon House books are available for special premiums and sales promotions as well as for fund-raising use. Special editions or book excerpts also can be created to specifications. For details, call 800.638.0928.

Disclaimer

Gryphon House, Inc., cannot be held responsible for damage, mishap, or injury incurred during the use of or because of activities in this book. Appropriate and reasonable caution and adult supervision of children involved in activities and corresponding to the age and capability of each child involved are recommended at all times. Do not leave children unattended at any time. Observe safety and caution at all times.

TABLE OF *Contents*

ACKNOWLEDGMENTS

I wish to express gratitude to everyone who was part of this joyful journey. I especially want to thank my husband, Brad, for his support and encouragement. Thanks to my children for their love and support and especially to my daughter Jenny for her feedback and proofreading skills. A great big thank you to my wonderful team who were part of this journey: Cathy Peshlakai, Sarah Wright, Rebecca Vizina, Janelle Jamero, Erin Skaggs, Robin Marx-Mackerley, Nikki Goldstein, Gigi Wynn, Lisa Whipple, Marisa LaCroix, Jen Gray, Sara Kharrat, Liz Blamire, Karina Levesque, Maddie Congdon, and Lori Ann Amian-Gabriel. Thanks to Stephanie Roselli and the editorial team at Gryphon House for all their expertise. Sincere thanks to all the leaders in the early childhood field who have enriched my life, shared their stories, and found the joyful leader within.

INTRODUCTION

Rise and Shine

Leaders determine how they will rise; they also empower others to shine.

A few years ago, Kim Raab, a child-care director at La Petite Academy, a private child-care facility in Las Vegas, Nevada, attended the Leadership of Community of Practice. I facilitate this group of professionals who regularly meet to discuss ideas and improve their practices. Kim shared the following:

> I have been in the early childhood field for the past twenty-eight years and an academy director for twenty-four of those years. A couple of years ago, I found myself in a place of wondering if there was something different that I should be doing. I was feeling as if I was doing the exact same thing each and every day, and to be honest with you, I was bored. I was looking for a change.
>
> It was during that time that I was told about the Leadership of Community of Practice. It sounded fantastic, but I was hesitant about joining the group as it was totally out of my comfort zone. I am not one who is comfortable going into unfamiliar situations and putting myself out there, but I knew that I needed something. I needed to do something for me. Furthermore, I needed to see if staying in early childhood education as a leader was really where I needed to be, or if it was my time to move on.
>
> Walking through those doors on the first day was one of the best decisions I have ever made. It is hard to put into words exactly what this course has done for me, but the best way I can describe it is that it has literally changed my life. I know that may seem a little over the top, but this class has reassured me that I am exactly where I need to be. It gave me the final push to complete my college degree. It has made me a better leader to my team and has given me a new love for the early childhood education field.

> In the two years that I have attended the Leadership of Community of Practice, I have received two prestigious awards within our company. I was honored with the People Leadership Award in 2020 and the Diamond Director in 2021. These are two of the highest awards that are given out to academy directors within our company. I am extremely humbled by these awards and have to thank the Leadership of Community of Practice for giving me the motivation, inspiration, confidence, and support to find myself again. I became a joyful leader.

Kim regained her motivation and confidence when she had opportunities to discuss challenges with other early childhood leaders and brainstorm solutions with them. She realized that other directors were facing similar issues and that she wasn't alone in her struggles. Kim left the Leadership of Community of Practice sessions feeling encouraged and less isolated. Over time, she recaptured her purpose and became a joyful leader.

You may be able to relate to how Kim felt. Have you ever asked yourself if you are in the right place, doing the right thing? You may have wondered if you were making a difference and being an effective leader. As a leader, you will undoubtedly face many challenges. You may be feeling symptoms of burnout, but you also have opportunities to be a positive influence on the individuals you lead.

In this book, we will be exploring aspects of joyful leadership. My hope is that you will discover the joyful leader within yourself, and then help others do the same. Going on a joyful leadership journey can positively change your life and transform your leadership.

JOYFUL LEADERSHIP

What is joyful leadership? It is uplifting, guiding, and inspiring others with a joyful spirit. Even if you do not have an official leadership position, you can still lead with joy. Early childhood teachers who guide children in their play and joyfully engage with them are leaders of their classroom. Early childhood coaches who support and inspire teachers to enhance their teaching practices are leaders in improving quality. Children who befriend other children and are kind to them are leaders in their classroom. If you are an individual who uplifts, guides, and inspires others with joy, then you are a joyful leader!

Being a joyful leader is not a one-time event; it is an ongoing journey of intentionally bringing joy to your work, whether you're planning a meeting or leading children in daily learning experiences. I have seen many early childhood teachers who are joyful leaders. They bring joy to their classroom and delight in spending time with children. Their classrooms are filled with laughter and smiles. These teachers joyfully encourage and influence others through their actions. They brighten the lives of children, families, coworkers, and colleagues by building meaningful relationships. Joyful teachers intentionally offer children opportunities for growth and development as they explore their world. These teachers meet each day with joy in their hearts as they empower others to shine. They rise and shine.

RISE AND SHINE

What does it mean to rise and shine? *To rise* is an upward movement. Think about a hot-air balloon: the air causes the balloon to rise because hot air is lighter than the surrounding colder air. When the sun rises in the morning, it lights up the sky and is a joyful sight. Joyful leaders elevate negative thoughts and actions with positive, joyful ones. They rise to the occasion as they live their purpose and empower others to do the same.

To shine is to give out a bright light or to have a quality of brightness. The sun shines on the Earth and provides life-giving light, which is an essential element of growth. When individuals shine, they have distinguished themselves or excelled at something. Leaders give individuals opportunities to shine by highlighting their brightness and accomplishments. They honor the gifts and talents of the individuals they lead; they let their light shine.

The expression "rise and shine" is often used to wish someone happiness as they wake up. It encourages the individual to get up, be joyful, and have a great day. Likewise, leaders can encourage their team to go forth, be happy, and have a productive day. Children are happier in classrooms with teachers who are joyful. Workers are more contented in workplaces that focus on strengths. Leaders are more effective when they elevate their team members. Positivity can make a difference in your relationships and your productivity. When we feel joyful, life seems better, and we are less prone to burnout. Joyful leaders are able to accomplish more because they have higher levels of energy and motivation.

HOW TO USE THIS BOOK

In this book we explore many ways that a joyful leader can rise and help others shine. To begin our journey, we will look at why joy is an essential element of effective leadership. We will then explore five aspects of joyful leadership:

- Reimagine Your Purpose
- Radiate a Joyful Outlook
- Engage in Joyful Actions
- Create Caring Connections
- Use Reflection to Build Strengths

Throughout this book, you will find ideas on how you can *rise now* by implementing strategies to help you become a more joyful leader (look for the icon). You'll also find ways to *shine on* the individuals that you lead and inspire them to be more joyful (look for the icon).

Interspersed throughout each chapter are real-life examples of leaders and teachers leading with joy. (The names of the teachers and children are pseudonyms to protect their privacy.) Each chapter concludes with discussion questions, a reflection activity, and an action plan so you and your team members can reflect on the chapter's content and put the ideas into action. If you are using this book as part of training or professional development, consider creating a Joyful Leader Book Club (see appendix A) in which your team reads, reflects, and then acts on what they learn in each chapter.

As I became a more joyful leader, it wasn't long before I was leading a more joyful team. My work became more meaningful. I developed stronger relationships with my team members, and we engaged in more joyful actions. Our creativity increased and we were able to face challenges with more fortitude and unity. We focused on what we could change, and we let go of what we could not change. We supported each other during hard times and celebrated joyful moments. It's worth noting that focusing on joy and finding the joyful leader within does not mean having toxic positivity. *Toxic positivity* is the belief that people should maintain a positive mindset regardless of the situation (Cherry, 2023). Everyone experiences hard times and painful experiences. When you feel negative emotions, you need to experience and deal with them, not suppress them or pretend they do not exist. Negative emotions are a part of life, and they need to be acknowledged and validated.

Joyful and effective leaders recognize that it is okay to not be okay. When experiencing difficult times and emotions, lean on others for support. Share your true feelings and recognize they are real and valid. Accept and process your emotions in healthy ways. Within this book, I will share times when I experienced difficult situations that were not joyful. I will also share how being a joyful leader helped me bounce back and move forward. As Ingrid Fetell Lee, author of *Joyful: The Surprising Power of Ordinary Things to Create Extraordinary Happiness*, shared on Instagram (2022), "In the middle of a crisis, remember that joy always comes back. You don't have to smile through the tough stuff or remind yourself it could've been so much worse. You're allowed to feel disappointed, frustrated, or pissed off. But, if you can, try to remember that joy always comes back. When you keep yourself open to the possibility of joy in the future, you make it more likely you'll notice it when it returns."

Remember, after experiencing tough times, joy will come back, and you can again find the joyful leader within. As you do, your team members will discover the joyful leader within themselves and become joyful influences on others. Together, you will weather both the good times and the not-so-good times. Joyful leadership is a journey, not a destination. You are invited to join me as I share how I became a more joyful leader, leading a joyful team.

CHAPTER 1

Why Joy?

"You can't go back and change the beginning, but you can start where you are and change the ending."

—*C.S. Lewis,* British author and scholar (attributed)

You rise as a leader as you infuse joy into your leadership. Have you ever had a moment or event that changed your life and started you on a different path? I had one when I was introduced to the work of Ingrid Fetell Lee. In 2018, one of my team members invited me to watch Lee's TED Talk called "Where Joy Hides and How to Find It." During her talk, Lee describes a personal experience that started her on a quest to find more about joy. Her professor was viewing her design work and told her that it brought him a feeling of joy, which surprised her as she had been focused on making her designs practical, ergonomic, and sustainable.

Lee began her quest by asking people about what things brought them joy. Some of the common responses she heard included rainbows, bubbles, cherry blossoms, and fireworks. She wondered, "Why do fireworks cause us to ooh and ahh?" "What makes looking at rainbows a joyful experience for almost everyone?" As she looked at pictures of things that individuals found joyful, she started to see some patterns. People often experienced joyful sensations when they saw things that were round, colorful, and surprising. Hot-air balloons and things that give a sense of abundance or feelings of lightness and elevation were seen as joyful. As Lee aptly shared, one *confetto*, the singular form of the word *confetti*, is not nearly as joyful as hundreds of pieces of confetti! After ten years of study and thought, Lee wrote *Joyful: The Surprising Power of Ordinary Things to Create Extraordinary Happiness*, which describes her findings on joy.

JOY

Lee's TED Talk and book inspired me to think about joy and how it could be an important aspect of leadership. I wanted to become a more joyful leader and was curious about discovering more about the following:

* What is joy?
* What brings me joy?
* What type of things do others find joyful?

WHAT IS JOY?

Joy can be described as moments when you spontaneously see or hear something that causes you to feel delighted. Lee describes it as "intense momentary experience of positive emotions." In contrast, happiness is how good you feel over time; it is feeling a sense of satisfaction and contentment with your life. Brené Brown, author of *The Gifts of Imperfection* suggests to her readers a familiar joyful symbol. "Twinkling lights are the perfect metaphor for joy," she writes. "Joy is not a constant. It comes to us in moments—often ordinary moments. Sometimes, we miss out on the bursts of joy because we're too busy chasing down extraordinary moments. Other times we're so afraid of the dark that we don't dare let ourselves enjoy the light. I believe a joyful life is made up of joyful moments gracefully strung together by trust, gratitude, inspiration, and faith."

"Joy is not a distant destination in which you arrive, but a path you choose to travel each day!"

—Tommy Newberry, author and speaker

To be joyful is to have feelings of delight or bliss. Joy often begins with the senses, or what Lee calls the aesthetics of joy. By being more aware of the aesthetics of joy and where to find them, you can discover many joyful things throughout your day. Take a moment to join me in the following visualization:

* Take a deep breath and clear your mind.
* Imagine something that makes you feel joyful. It could be a person, place, or thing.
* Become aware of how you are feeling. Continue to breathe deeply.
* Think about where you are. What are you seeing? hearing? smelling? touching? tasting? Think about each sense that you are experiencing.
* Allow the sensations of the experience to flow throughout your whole body.
* Savor how you are feeling. Enjoy being at this moment.

* Imprint the moment in your mind and your heart. Continue thinking about your joyful thoughts and feelings.
* (Wait at least one minute.) When you are ready, slowly open your eyes.
* How did you feel? Write down your thoughts and feelings.

Becoming more mindful of joyful experiences and thinking about them often is one way to become more joyful. Joyful experiences help us feel good about ourselves and others.

WHAT BRINGS ME JOY?

My next question was "What brings me joy?" I thought about the joy I feel when I spend time with my family and friends. I also thought about the types of things that bring me joy within my surroundings. I became more intentional about noticing details that I found joyful, called *joyspotting* (see page 12 for more on this topic). One day on my drive to work, I saw a large yellow balloon floating high above a new neighborhood. As it floated in the breeze in the blue, blue sky with wispy white clouds in the background, I felt joyful. I noticed some purple and pink flowers that I had not seen before blooming in a neighbor's yard, and they brought a smile to my face. Noticing balloons and flowers was a simple action and yet when I arrived at work, I felt more joyful and wanted to share my joy with others. As I shared my observations, others responded by sharing something that brought them joy. There was a snowball effect as more people began sharing their joy with each other.

Over time, I discovered that being more mindful of joy improved my life, work, and well-being. When I feel better, I am more creative. When I make mental and emotional shifts toward being more joyful, I improve my productivity. I am less likely to feel burned out, and this positively affects the people I lead.

WHAT TYPES OF THINGS DO OTHERS FIND JOYFUL?

As I became more joyful, my team became more joyful, and their productivity increased. This led me to my third question, "What types of things do others find joyful?" As Lee discovered, some things, such as fireworks, are almost universally joyful, but individuals might find joy in specific things, such as a hand-drawn picture created by their son or daughter. My team found joy in having opportunities to be creative and interact collaboratively within a positive work environment. They enjoyed working together and learning more about each other professionally and personally.

"I've learned that people will forget what you said, people will forget what you did, but people will never forget how you made them feel."

—**Maya Angelou,** author, poet, and civil rights activist

FINDING JOY AMIDST STRUGGLES

Although it may be easy to find joy when things are going our way, we all know that life doesn't work that way. We all have struggles—both personal and professional. On a personal level, you may find it hard to feel joy when you are anxious or stressed. Some people feel guilty expressing joy during difficult times, yet joy can help us recover from the physiological effects of stress and burnout. In fact, joy can provide respite during tough times and make us more resilient. Evelyn Ritzi, Content Marketing Manager at The Ohlman Group, shared that when we are faced with difficulties, instead of bouncing back, we should focus on bouncing forward. Bouncing forward means not just to get back up after falling down, but to get up and jump forward over or through what knocked us down in the first place. Ritzi suggested that one way to bounce forward is to find meaning in adversity by noticing and celebrating small moments of joy. Experiencing joy can help us recover from stress, anxiety, and negative feedback loops. As we find purpose and meaning, we will become more resilient and better able to bounce forward.

One helpful action that can help you bounce forward is to pause for a few moments and think about something that you are thankful for or something that has brought you joy in the past. Although stopping to pause and focus on joy for a few moments does not change your circumstances, it can change how you feel. Focusing on joy can help reset your brain to a more positive mindset and return to an upward spiral.

- Pause and focus on something for which you are thankful.
- Encourage your team to share something for which they are thankful.

On a professional level, whether you are the teacher leading a group of children or a director leading a team of teachers, some days will be difficult: a staff member calls in sick, a child has a meltdown, or a licensing agency shows up for a surprise inspection. However, if we look for it, we can find joy during struggles. You can find joy as you listen to children laugh as they play or as you think of a joyful memory. Joy is a choice. Each day, we make choices about what we will say and do. When events occur, we have a choice in how we will respond. Our responses can make a big difference in the outcome of a situation.

"The day I decided my life was joyful, there was suddenly joy all around me."

—Anonymous

Let me share a personal example. Before becoming a joyful leader, my response to situations was often different from what they are today. In the past, when I faced a challenge such as a cut in funding, I focused on all the possible negative outcomes. Likewise, I would sometimes avoid addressing the issue as I didn't want to upset the individuals who would be affected. I was also fearful that if I told staff about the potential budget cuts, they would leave the organization and find other positions. My reaction of fear, worry, and avoidance often resulted in the very things that I was trying to avoid. It wasn't long before my team picked up on my negative emotions and rumors started to spread. My team began to exhibit fear and worry. The outcome was a negative work climate and team members looking for employment elsewhere. Recently, I faced a similar situation, but my response changed, and the outcome was very different because of my joyful mindset.

> I oversee several grants that provide funding for training and coaching early childhood educators. A few years ago, I learned that one of my contracts might not be renewed because of state budget cuts. The funding cuts would directly affect the positions of two of my team members. Instead of being overcome with fear and worry and avoiding the situation, I responded differently. I met with my team and explained the situation with an optimistic outlook. I emphasized that I thought we had the creative energy to think of different ways we could approach this situation. I shared that I had given them the worst-case scenario and that funding might not be cut, but we needed to start exploring other options if it was cut. We brainstormed many different ideas, including approaching my supervisor about finding a different source of funding to carry us over until we knew the actual outcome. With a positive and joyful attitude, I met with my supervisor and outlined the situation. I emphasized the positive effect my team members were having on the early childhood community and asked him what he could do. To my surprise, he offered to cover the salaries of the staff members for three months, or until we knew the outcome of the funding. He shared that he had been impressed by my team and that he never had to worry about them getting their work done. He also mentioned that my team seemed happy and never came to him with issues. Wow! A few months later, we received even better news when we learned that we were not only funded for another year but at a higher level of funding!

This was one of those times when I was grateful that I had become a joyful leader and that I was leading a joyful team. Each day, early childhood professionals determine how they will respond to a situation or event. The response greatly influences the outcome. This can especially be true in early childhood classrooms, as Erica discovered:

> Tommy was a new child in Erica's preschool classroom. On his first day, Tommy displayed some challenging behavior that was dangerous to the other children. Erica learned that he was facing several challenges at home and needed extra care and attention. When Tommy was feeling anxious, he would shout at his teachers and the other children, throw toys, and sometimes even kick and punch the teachers when they tried to intervene. The teachers consistently gave Tommy positive care and attention and did their best to minimize his anxiety.
>
> One morning, while on the playground, Tommy began swearing and throwing toys. The teachers moved the other children away from him and gave him some space to express his emotions. Erica started to talk to him quietly and calmly. She invited him to go into the quiet, empty classroom with her. As she moved closer to him, he ran into the classroom, hid behind the dollhouse, and began throwing the dolls at her. Erica crouched down and said, "I know you're having big feelings right now. Would you like me to sit with you or give you some space?" Tommy didn't respond verbally, he just continued throwing the dolls. Erica said, "I'm going to move over here and play with some bean bags, and you can let me know if you want me to come back." After Erica moved away, Tommy stopped throwing the dolls and began crying. Erica wanted to scoop him up in a hug, but she knew that would only upset him more. She said, "Would you like to come over here and play with the bean bags?" Tommy stopped crying and a few minutes later said, "Yes." Erica asked Tommy where he would like to throw the bean bags, and he said that he wanted to throw them to her outside.

> Erica and Tommy went back outside to play catch, and his expression and demeanor completely changed. He had the biggest smile on his face. He began doing spins as he threw the bean bags, throwing them backwards over his head, closing his eyes and throwing them, and laughing the whole time. Erica shared his enthusiasm and commented positively on his creative throwing skills. Soon some other children began to show interest in the game and a few asked if they could participate. Tommy said they could join them, and three children started throwing bean bags in creative ways. He seemed so proud of himself whenever he would catch a bean bag from one of the other children. Tommy continued to do well the rest of the day, and he eagerly talked about how much fun he had playing with the bean bags.

Erica's response to Tommy's challenging behavior led to a positive outcome. She was a joyful leader, making a positive difference in the lives of the children in her class.

Joyful leaders can set the tone for how others will act and react. Your responses to situations, especially difficult ones, influence how your team or children in your classroom will react. Not all situations will turn out the way you want them to, but by being a joyful leader, you will be better able to address each situation positively.

JOYFUL LEADERS

- lift others and spread joy;
- help others be the best versions of themselves;
- are present and actively listen with intent;
- strive to make joyful connections with others;
- are encouraging, offering positive viewpoints;
- have a sense of playfulness and fun with the individuals they lead; and
- are aware that they will face daily struggles, but that there will also be moments of joy.

MY JOURNEY

As noted previously, joy was not always an essential part of my leadership. I had to make a big shift in my outlook and communication. It took time and intentional actions, but I've become a joyful leader leading a joyful team. I share my journey here to inspire you to start your own journey on becoming a joyful leader.

> I lead a team of seventeen early childhood professionals, including trainers, coaches, assessors, and an administrative assistant. After hearing and learning more about Lee's work on joy, I wanted to adopt a more joyful attitude and to share what I had learned with my team. As I prepared for an upcoming team retreat, I developed a short presentation on joy. I encouraged my staff to share three things that brought them joy. During our retreat, I also invited my team members to share a story about a time they felt joy. As they shared their stories, their faces lit up, and they were truly joyful!
>
> We discussed how we could bring more joy into our work with early childhood professionals. One idea was to create training presentations on topics related to joy, such as "The Joyful Teacher" and "Bringing More Joy into Early Childhood Classrooms" that we could teach to early childhood educators. I encouraged everyone to notice little moments of joy and to share these experiences with each other. When we became more attuned to seeing joyful things in the world, our spirits were lifted, and we became more observant. We found that sharing our joy with others helped them feel more joyful.

Think for a moment: What brings you joy?

- Write down three things that bring you joy.
- Ask your team members or children in your classroom to share three things that bring them joy.

JOYSPOTTING

The more I learned about joy, the more I started to recognize joyful things in my environment. I started intentionally looking for things. I noticed a bunny hopping in my yard and saw some amazing artwork during a weekend trip. I was joyspotting. Lee (2019b) describes *joyspotting* as tuning your attention to joy in your surroundings. It is noticing someone's polka-dotted socks or the colorful butterfly flitting among the plants. Joyspotting can positively influence how you feel. Why does joyspotting work? According to Lee (2019a), "One reason might have to do with what positivity researchers call upward spirals. It turns out that emotions have feedback loops: when we feel a burst of joy, it makes us more attentive to joy in our surroundings and more likely to engage in behaviors that help us find more joy, such as interacting with other people or doing an activity we love." I have found that joyspotting has created an upward spiral within my team. Noticing joyful things in our environment has helped us be more joyful.

My team started texting each other pictures of things they found joyful. Several team members commented on how the word *joy* popped out at them wherever they went. One team member was shopping and saw some word tiles that read "Choose Joy." She said as soon as she saw the tiles, she knew she needed to buy one for everyone on our team. Another member of the team created personalized whiteboards for team members that included a picture of one of the things that brought them joy. My board had a picture of a purple iris (my favorite flower). Other boards featured hummingbirds, cherry blossoms, and a pineapple.

Interested in joyspotting? I found some great ideas on where to look for joy in Lee's "The Joyspotter's Guide," which can be found on her website. The guide lists twelve ideas on where to look for joy. Here are four ideas to get you started:

- **Look up!** When I looked up, I saw beautiful light fixtures at a hotel and a restaurant.
- **Look down!** When I looked down, I saw a fun sidewalk mosaic featuring sea life.
- **Keep an eye out for color.** When I kept an eye out for color, I came upon some sculptures in vibrant jewel-tone hues.
- **Zoom in.** When I zoomed in, I saw the most amazing papier-mâché animal figures in the window display of a children's art museum.

Start joyspotting, and share joyspotting ideas with your team.

Encourage your team to start joyspotting and to share their joyspotting with each other.

BECOMING A JOYFUL LEADER

As mentioned earlier, you do not need an official title to be a leader. When individuals guide and inspire with joy, they become joyful leaders. Throughout this book, I will be referring to the individuals that you lead as your "team." Whether your team is teachers you supervise or children you teach, you can be a joyful leader leading a joyful team. Please replace the word *team* with whatever term best matches your situation. Your team may be students, parents, teachers, coaches, trainers, or other individuals you influence. Think of your "team" as we explore different aspects of joyful leadership.

As I became a joyful leader, it felt good to focus on joy, and I began infusing joy into everything I did. I changed the name of the icebreakers I implemented during training sessions to Joyful Beginnings (more about this later in this book). My team began looking at our surroundings at work and thinking about how we could make them more joyful. We started setting up joyful environments for meetings and training sessions, which increased the energy and excitement in the room. For example, we added items such as sunflowers, seashells, and decorative birdhouses. My team and I looked deeper at the concept of joy and began discussing topics such as creating joyful connections with others, building more joyful relationships, and being a joyful influence on others. Over time, joy became part of our team culture and an integral part of who we were, both personally and professionally. Does that mean that everything we did was joyful? Of course not. We still faced times of discouragement and disappointment, but we were able to face the hard days with resilience and adapt to our difficult circumstances. We remembered that joy would come back, and it did.

The wonderful thing about joy is that it does not cost anything and is something that can be readily shared. As my team felt more joy, they wanted to share the message of joy and gratitude with the individuals they teach. One of my team members was working with a group of preschool teachers over a series of several months. The teachers would come to their evening classes tired, often hungry, and not always in the best of moods. She gave the teachers a joy journal and invited them to write down one thing or experience that had brought them joy that day. Then, several teachers were invited to share their joy with the class. At first, the teachers grumbled and not many of them wanted to share; however, over time, they became more excited about writing in their joy journals and were eager to share their joy. The teachers' "joy-finding mental muscle" had been strengthened, and they were noticing joyful moments in their day: they were learning how to be more joyful leaders in their classrooms.

As I spread joy to others, it came back to me two-fold. My team and the people I teach began sharing their joy with me. A colleague sent me a card thanking me for helping her find more joy in her role as a leader. She shared that she had become a more joyful leader by following my example and implementing strategies she had been taught.

One of my team members recently sent me a photo of a beautiful bird, resplendent with my favorite colors. It was a simple gesture, yet it brought me lots of joy (it brings me joy thinking about it now). Once you have found joy within yourself, joy starts rippling outward to your family, friends, team, and the many people who cross your path each day. Joy is a powerful connector that touches hearts and minds.

It was through these experiences and many more that I emerged as a joyful leader leading a joyful team. I was seeing the positive impact that joyful leadership was having us. That is why I strongly believe that joy is an essential element of effective leadership.

DISCUSSION QUESTIONS

1. How could infusing joy into your leadership influence the individuals you lead?

2. How can you change your mindset when faced with a struggle?

3. How could you incorporate the idea of joyspotting into team meetings or your classroom?

4. What are some benefits of having joy as an essential element of leadership?

REFLECTION ACTIVITY: 3, 2, 1

* Describe three ideas that you want to remember.

___

___

___

* List two things that you want to do.

___

___

___

* Write down one question you would like to discuss with others.

___

___

___

ACTION PLAN

Determine one or more actions you will take this month that focus on joy.

- Action:

  ____

  ____

  ____

- Why is this action important?

  ____

  ____

  ____

- What are my next steps?

  ____

  ____

  ____

CHAPTER 2

Reimagine Your Purpose

"When you choose joy you feel good, and when you feel good you do good, and when you do good it reminds others of what joy feels like, and it just might inspire them to do the same."

—*Sherri Bishop*, IncredibleJoy.com

I really love the word *reimagine*. You rise as a leader as you reimagine your purpose. To *reimagine* means to rethink or re-create. Reimagining is changing the way you look at something and interpreting it. Consider the following: You are house hunting, and you visit a house that needs some TLC. As you go from room to room, you look beyond the current state of the rooms and reimagine what it could look like with a little work, a touch of new paint, lots of new carpet, and your own furniture. Although the structure remains the same, you are thinking about how you can personalize and enhance the space to match your preferences and style. You reimagine the space and how you could transform it.

Likewise, you can reimagine your leadership. You can rethink or re-create what you are doing by digging deeper and imagining how things could be with a little work, a touch of joy, lots of commitment, and your own leadership style. Reimagine yourself as a more joyful leader, leading a joyful team. What would be different? What would be the same?

Say the following phrase aloud, "I am a joyful leader, and I lead a joyful team." Were you comfortable saying those words, or did it feel awkward? If you felt awkward, you are not alone. It can feel awkward to change how you view your leadership, and this chapter will help you through this process. You'll learn how to discover and live your purpose, and then learn to lead as your team reimagines and lives their purpose.

DISCOVERING YOUR PURPOSE

One of the first steps in the process of becoming a joyful leader is to define your purpose as it relates to your leadership. Your purpose is your vision of who you want to be and what you want to do. It can be a driving force in how you choose to use your time and energy. Defining your purpose is important because it describes the impact that you want to make as a leader. Your purpose offers direction, guides your words and actions, and helps you focus on what matters to you.

You may already have a clear idea of your purpose, but if you do not, you may be wondering, "How do I discover my purpose?" This takes thoughtful consideration. It may be helpful to think about what type of impact you want to make as a leader. Valorie Burton (2018), founder of the Coaching and Positive Psychology Institute, suggests we ask ourselves, "How is someone's life better when they cross paths with me?" I have thought deeply about this question and determined that I wanted the individuals who cross my path to experience joy during our interactions. This led to a deep dive into learning more about the feeling of joy and how to help others feel more of it. After much reflection, I determined that my purpose—my why—is to elevate others and inspire them to joyfully follow their purpose and passion.

- Reflect on your response to the question, "How is someone's life better when they cross paths with me?" As you contemplate your answer, identify and define your purpose.
- Ask your team members to reflect on "How is someone's life better when they cross paths with me?" As they contemplate their answer, invite them to identify and define their purpose.

Thinking about your why or your purpose can reshape your work as a leader. Reflect on what motivates you to get up and look forward to the day ahead. Your why (purpose) will make your what (being a leader) more effective. Your why is much more important than your what. We are motivated by our whys. If you are still struggling to determine your purpose, try asking yourself the 5 Whys.

THE 5 WHYS

In the 1930s, Sakichi Toyoda, a Japanese inventor, industrialist, and founder of Toyota Industries, developed the "5 Whys," a strategy that Toyota still uses today (Kanbanize, n.d.). The premise of the strategy is that by asking *Why* five times, the problem and the solution become clearer. Depending on the problem, you may need to ask why more or fewer times than five. It is important to keep asking why until you identify the core concept.

You can determine your purpose by asking yourself why five times. This strategy can help you to dig deeper as you determine your purpose. Let's look at an example.

What is my purpose or *why do I do what I do?* My purpose is to create positive change and improve quality in early childhood education.

Why? To build community within each school and classroom

Why? To support teachers in achieving positive outcomes

Why? To give young children a safe and nurturing environment

Why? To support families and promote the optimum growth and development of their children

What is my purpose? To create positive change by supporting families and promoting the optimum growth and development of young children

By asking the 5 Whys, the purpose became clearer. It required digging deeper into the many facets of why I do what I do. You can also use the 5 Whys to determine core issues to problems such as challenging behavior by a child in an early childhood classroom.

- Ask yourself, "What is my purpose?" or "Why do I do what I do?" five times and then write down your purpose.
- Encourage your team members to ask themselves "What is my purpose?" or "Why do I do what I do?" five times and then write down their purpose.

Gaining a deeper understanding of your purpose will sustain you when you are facing difficult circumstances. When challenges arise, and they will, if you have dug deep and determined a purpose with personal meaning, it will help you ride the waves of discouragement and disappointment. Your deeper, personal why will help you get back up and keep going after you have been knocked down.

"Living on purpose means doing what truly matters to you in alignment with your values and beliefs."

—Katrina Ruth, *The Katrina Ruth Show*

LIVING YOUR PURPOSE

Living your purpose helps you determine how you will show up each day, as it requires you to look ahead and imagine the possibilities. You live your purpose through daily actions. Living your purpose will take time, effort, and commitment. There will be obstacles to living your purpose, but remember to keep the long-term view. When faced with failure, challenges, and fears, focus on how you can overcome these deterrents. I love this quote from *The Joy of Leadership*: "Failure is an inescapable part of life and a critically important part of any successful life. We learn to walk by falling, to talk by babbling, to shoot a basket by missing, and to color the inside of a square by scribbling outside the box. Those who intensely fear failing end up falling short of their potential. We either learn to fail or we fail to learn" (Ben-Shahar and Ridgway, 2017).

OVERCOMING FEARS

Take time to reflect on what could get in your way or cause you to get stuck when reimagining and living your purpose. Often the answer is related to some type of fear. The four most common types of fear are fear of failure, of success, of losing control or facing uncertainty, and fear of disapproval or rejection (Burton, 2022). These fears can stop us in our tracks and prevent us from moving forward and taking action.

If fears are preventing you from living your purpose, name them. I struggle with the fear of failure and fear of disapproval or rejection. By naming my fears, I have been able to start combating them. Also acknowledge your successes and use positive self-talk. For example, I will often use positive self-talk such as, "I am afraid of failing, but I also know failing can lead to opportunities to learn and grow. I have been successful in the past, and I will be successful again in the future. Furthermore, I will not let my fears prevent me from giving my best effort. I can do this."

When I use positive self-talk and think about past successes, my thinking shifts into a more positive mindset. In addition to using positive self-talk, I'm intentional about living my purpose each day, which has helped me overcome many of my fears. When I am focused on elevating others, my thoughts shift from myself to someone else, and my fear of disapproval slips away. I have found it beneficial to concentrate on what I can do right now, at this moment. I may not be able to solve the problem immediately, but I can reassure those around me that we will come up with a solution together.

"Most of us are afraid and brave at the exact same moment. All day long. Everyday."

—**Brené Brown** (2013)

After you have determined your purpose and thought about how to conquer possible obstacles, it is even more important to let your purpose drive how you live and lead each day. Winning the moment is one way to do this.

WINNING THE MOMENT

Think about your day. What has been the best moment so far? Did a child give you a hug? Did someone give you a word of encouragement or thanks? Were you excited that all your team came to work? What was your best moment? Each day is filled with moments or particular points in time. Some moments make an impression, and they become cherished memories. Other moments are forgettable. Many moments combined over time define who we are and what we are becoming.

To help me live my purpose, I have used an idea that Doshia Woods, head coach of the University of Denver women's basketball team, shared during Jon Gordon's 2021 Power of Positive Summit. She encourages her team to win the moment. This means being intentional and focusing on the present moment. It is making a conscious choice about what to say and do at that moment. For example, you can win the moment by taking time to say a kind word to someone. You can win the moment by putting down your phone and really being present as you listen to a friend, family member, co-worker, or child tell you about their day. Likewise, you can win the moment by tapping into your purpose.

Will you win all your moments? No, but each moment that you win can increase your overall joy and happiness. Sometimes, it is simply enough to brave the moment. One particularly hard moment that I had to brave was when I learned that my son had been in an auto accident and was being taken by life flight to the children's hospital. Time seemed to stop at that moment. Confusion, disbelief, and panic all set in. The drive to the hospital was never ending, and the many moments of watching my son fight for his life were terrifying. When you are faced with life-changing moments, you win the moment as you brave the moment. I had to be brave and find strength from deep within myself to face this very difficult situation. I had to be willing to face the unknown with courage I didn't think I possessed.

My family faced many moments that required bravery as my son started the long road of recovery from his injuries, which included traumatic brain injury. His healing process took more than fifteen years, and we had to brave many moments, but we also won many by being thankful and focusing on each small step forward. Fortunately, my son is currently thriving personally and professionally. We won each moment by braving each moment. One moment turned into two moments, which turned into ten moments, and before we knew it, we had won hundreds of moments.

Teachers win the moment when they are kind and loving to a child experiencing difficulties, as seen in the following example.

> One afternoon, Charleise was assisting children with their afternoon snack. One three-year-old was feeling irritable and unhappy after waking up from a nap and told Charleise he only wanted graham crackers for snack. Unfortunately, the snack for the day was pretzels and peaches, not graham crackers. Charleise sat down next to the child and said, "I know graham crackers are your favorite. Can you tell me what you like about graham crackers?" The boy responded with a pout on his face, "They're crunchy!" Charleise said, "Pretzels are crunchy." The boy frowned and said, "But graham crackers are sweet!" Charleise answered, "Peaches are sweet! What would happen if you put the peaches on top of the pretzel and ate them both in one bite?" The boy looked at her quizzically and then put his peach slice on top of the pretzel and put it in his mouth. As he chewed the snack, he began to smile at Charleise. "It's yummy!" he said. He continued to smile and eat his snack. This teacher won the moment by digging deeper and responding to the needs of the child.

Teachers win the moment when they pivot from their planned lesson, share in the unexpected interest of a young child, and turn it into a learning moment. They take time to look at the bug, listen to the garbage truck, and find the lost toy. We win the moment when we thank our team for coming to work and making a difference in the lives of children and families.

Determine how you will win the moment by trying the following:

- Pause and think about your purpose.
- Focus on what you can do at this moment to live your purpose.
- Determine next steps.
- Use your inner strength, and act on your resolve.

Repeat this exercise with your team members.

LEADING YOUR TEAM

In this chapter, we've looked at how you can reimagine your purpose by defining it and then living it. In the remainder of this chapter, we'll look at how you can be a leader to your team as they reimagine and live their purpose. This begins with a challenge that's familiar to all leaders: figuring out how not to do it all.

LIGHTENING YOUR LOAD

Leaders face many demands on their time and energy. You may be like me: You start off the day determined to live your purpose, and before the clock strikes nine o'clock in the morning, your best-laid plans have been set aside because of unexpected issues and too many demands on your time. When I become overwhelmed and stressed, I struggle to just get through the day. Can any of you relate? One of the strategies that has helped me live my purpose has been to lighten my load.

Lightening your load almost seems counterintuitive. As leaders, we need to do more and be more, right? That premise can lead to burnout. Have you ever considered that lightening your load could actually be an essential leadership task? The key to effective leadership is not doing more, but rather doing the things that will have the greatest impact. If you are overburdened with nonessential tasks that are diminishing your ability to be an effective leader and live your purpose, you may need to lighten your load. If you are hanging onto worries and struggles, these burdens will become heavier over time.

You might have seen a professor or trainer illustrate this concept by holding up a glass of water and asking the students, "How heavy is this glass of water?" The students give several answers related to the actual weight of the glass of water. The professor or trainer states that regardless of the actual weight of the glass of water, it will feel heavier the longer you hold it up. A few minutes or even hours might not be too bad, but if you hold it up for days, it will feel heavier, and your arm will cramp and begin to feel numb, which will eventually cause you to drop the glass. The weight of the glass does not change, yet the longer you hold the glass, the heavier it feels.

Likewise, the longer leaders hold onto their stress and worries, the heavier those will become. The only way to lessen the load is to drop or lighten the load. Imagine you have been invited to go on your first overnight camping trip, and you will be backpacking to your destination. Your friends give you suggestions on the equipment and items you will need to take. You begin purchasing and gathering the items. As you pack, you add a few extra items that you think you might need.

The day of the trip arrives, and you travel to your starting point. At first the trail is level and smooth, but then it becomes steeper, and you begin to feel the weight of your pack. You start regretting adding some extra items. After a few hours, your group stops for lunch. You are happy to take off your pack and rest. One of your friends asks you how you are doing, and you confide that your pack is feeling rather heavy and you wish you could lighten your load. She asks if she can look in your pack. You agree, and as she looks through it, she shakes her head and laughs a little. She takes out several items including some duplicates. She suggests discarding a couple of the items in a trash receptacle and offers to carry a few in her backpack. You thank her, and then it is time to be on your way again. As you continue the hike, your load feels lighter, but it is still a struggle at times.

As you continue the hike, your friends share what they have learned about what is essential and nonessential to bring along while backpacking. During one of the stops, one of your friends helps you redistribute the weight of the items in your backpack and adjusts your pack into a more comfortable position. Your friends give you recommendations on their favorite hiking shoes and packs. Having the support and guidance of your friends lifts your spirits and makes the trip more enjoyable. After the trip, you look through your pack and identify additional items that you did not use and would not need to take on your next adventure. You also commit to spending more time breaking in your shoes and increasing your endurance prior to your next hike.

As leaders, we have a backpack full of tasks that we carry. Some tasks are essential, and others are not. Sometimes, we duplicate doing the tasks of others and need to readjust our expectations. To successfully lighten your load so you can lead with your purpose, consider the following strategies.

IDENTIFY AND ANALYZE YOUR WORKLOAD

First, list your most common tasks, such as supervising staff, keeping track of finances, or talking to families. Then, analyze each task by asking yourself the following questions:

* **Is this task useful?** Leaders sometimes engage in tasks that become habits, such as checking emails every ten minutes, but the tasks may not be useful.
* **Am I the only one who can do the task?** Can I delegate this to someone else? Or is there someone else who could be trained to do the task?
* **Is the task my work task?** Are you trying to do or redo the work of others? Falling into the trap of doing someone else's work can be particularly problematic if what you are doing does not improve or change the outcome. The time and energy spent on the task is time that could be better spent on something else.
* **What is the actual time frame in which the task needs to be completed?** Can the time frame be extended? If it can, and you spread the task over two weeks instead of one week, you are redistributing the weight of the task that needs to be accomplished.
* **What tasks should be my priority or primary responsibilities?** If you determine that mentoring and coaching staff is a priority, but you are struggling to find time to complete that task, lightening the load can free up time to focus on the tasks that you have identified as your priorities.
* **When is your prime time for completing work?** When do you do your best work? If you do your best work in the morning, schedule tasks that need your best efforts at that time.
* **What aspects of your work bring you joy or make you happy?** If rocking a baby brings you joy, find time each day to visit the infant room. If you enjoy watching children play outside, find time to go outside each day. Your load will feel lighter when you feel joyful.

TAKE ACTION

Once you have identified and analyzed your workload, it is time to act.

- **Prioritize and delegate.** As leaders, it is easy to become distracted from doing the most important task. When you become distracted, recognize that you are distracted and then refocus your attention and ask yourself, "What is most important?" If you are spending too much time on nonessential tasks, prioritize and schedule specific times to take care of things that have a lower priority later when you have less mental energy. Work on the most important tasks during your peak performance times. One director started her day by greeting staff and students as they arrived. She felt her best in the morning, and one of her priorities was developing meaningful relationships with staff and students. Afterward, she focused on taking care of other issues.

  You can also lighten your load by delegating tasks to others. You do not need to do everything. Determine which tasks are leadership and administrative tasks that need to be completed by you and which tasks could be completed by your team or others, such as parent volunteers. For example, if you have an upcoming event, instead of taking the lead on organizing and implementing the event, ask your team or others to undertake the task.

- **Visualize your best moments.** If you are feeling down and overwhelmed, think about your best moments as a leader. Create a photo board of joyful classroom moments, or write in a journal describing your best moments as a leader. Take time every day to visualize or read about some of your best moments. This action will remind you of your strengths, boost your confidence, and lighten your load.

- **Adjust the intensity.** When we're stressed, some actions can seem overwhelming. Instead of eliminating an action, lighten the load by looking for ways to adjust or decrease the intensity. Create a plan that breaks down the tasks into smaller actions that can be accomplished over a longer period of time. For example, instead of trying to complete all your staff or student evaluations in one week, spread them out over several weeks so the task feels less overwhelming.

- **Create a network of support.** Surround yourself with individuals who will support and encourage you in your efforts. We can all benefit from having our own personal cheering squad that will lift us up when we are down and help us through discouraging times. By establishing a network of support, we can gain strength from others, and we have opportunities to give strength to them. Find a few close associates that you can confide in who will provide you with an unbiased listening ear. Rely on your network of support to help you through difficult times, and commit to doing the same for them. Let others know when you need assistance, and always express gratitude for the help they provide.

* **Set up a joyful environment.** Your mental and physical environment matters. What you think about and what you see in your surroundings make a difference in how you feel and how you act. Within a classroom, create a display of things that you and the children find joyful. Your joy meter will rise as you surround yourself with joyful things. See chapter 4 for ideas on designing a joyful environment.

* **View work as a gift.** It is a gift to be able to work and be a leader. Focus on positive outcomes and how you can make a difference. Our perspective can make a big difference in how we feel and behave. You may feel a sense of accomplishment and feel excited about the work you are doing, or you may feel sad or upset because things did not turn out the way you expected. Viewing work as a gift will increase your feelings of self-worth and accomplishment. You will feel a greater appreciation for your efforts and value your contribution as a leader, which, in turn, will help lighten your load.

* **Increase your ability.** By becoming more efficient or effective in your abilities, you can lighten your load. Take classes to learn new skills, or create or join a leadership community of practice. As you strengthen yourself and increase your confidence, you will be able to figure out ways to carry your load more effectively.

Now that we have identified several strategies for lightening your load, it is time to go on your leadership backpacking adventure. Begin by identifying all the tasks you think you will need to accomplish or take on your adventure. Load your leadership backpack and start your hike. As your leadership load becomes heavier, start determining which tasks you can eliminate or discard. Ask others to carry part of the load by delegating tasks and training others to take them on. As you climb the leadership mountain, focus on your strengths and past successes. Do not climb the mountain alone; surround yourself with friends and colleagues who will encourage and support you in your efforts. As you take additional trips, continue to increase your knowledge and skills. Learn how to complete tasks more effectively and efficiently. Slow down and stop along the way so that you can enjoy the view. Spread your trip over a longer time frame so that you do not feel rushed or overwhelmed. Create a joyful environment, and view your leadership opportunity as a gift. As you do these things, your load will be lighter, and you will find joy in your leadership journey.

Determine one way that you can lighten your load, and act on your idea.

Give your team opportunities to shine as they take the lead on activities and events.

"Attaining lasting happiness requires that we enjoy the journey on our way toward a destination we deem valuable. Happiness is not about making it to the peak of the mountain, nor is it about climbing aimlessly around the mountain; happiness is the experience of climbing toward the peak."

—Ben-Shahar and Ridgway (2017)

ONE-WORD JOURNEYS

Just as it is important for leaders to determine and live their purpose, it is also important for each member of your team to determine and live their purpose. A one-word journey is one way that I have guided my team to reimagine their purpose.

Authors Jon Gordon, Dan Britton, and Jimmy Page (2013), in their book *One Word That Will Change Your Life*, propose that instead of making New Year's resolutions, which are often unfulfilled, carefully select one word that will become the driving force for who you want to be in the year ahead. To find your word, the authors recommend that you first "look in" to your heart and find a word that resonates with your being. Then, you "look up" to receive inspiration in finding your word. Finally, you "look out" and see how your word will help you live better. Finding your one word can come quickly or take much thought and reflection. For example, in 2018, my one word was *engagement*. I was in the midst of writing my book *Lose the Lecture: Engaging Approaches to Early Childhood Professional Learning*, and I was focused on increasing the engagement of learners participating in professional learning experiences. The word *engagement* became a driving force for my professional work that year. It influenced how I interacted with others and what I focused on as a leader. As I let my word be my driving force, I found power in living my one word.

- Select one word that will be your driving force for the year.

GUIDE YOUR TEAM TO FIND THEIR ONE WORD

Guiding your team to find their one word can help them reimagine their purpose. At a team meeting, I shared how I had determined my one word and how it was making a positive difference in my life. I asked them if they were interested in finding their own one word. They were, and so I challenged them to take time to do that before our next team meeting. When we met again, everyone was invited to share.

Team members' one words included *blossom, awakening, grow, forward, trust, confidence, vulnerability,* and *quiet*. I invited them to share why they had selected their word. Here are two of their responses.

Nikki shared that she had chosen the word *awakening*. She said that for several years she has been preparing her heart to be ready to do the work that fulfills her purpose. This had included many deep dives into self-care and self-love, as well as finding comfort and complete trust in faith and hope. She shared that although she was not yet entirely awakened to what her purpose was, she knew that her heart was prepared to do work in service to others. She hoped during the year to become fully awakened to what she was uniquely made to do by laying the groundwork, following the leads, and preparing for the arrival of her purpose.

Sarah shared that she had chosen the word *grow* because she had undergone many changes in her life recently and had struggled with finding a word that would capture the positive side of things she was going through. She chose her word because she knew she needed to continue to grow in many ways. She wanted to learn new ways to engage adult learners.

She planned on growing as she took on new projects. She said she would encourage others to grow as she acted as a mentor and a coach. She believed this word would be powerful in her life because sometimes growth can be difficult, but it is also possible to grow in different directions.

- Invite your team to select their one word for the year.

Sharing your one word with others can be an emotional experience because the word you choose has such deep and personal meaning. Your one-word journey can bring you joy as you see yourself transformed by the experience. One of the recommendations Gordon, Britton, and Page (2013) suggest is to have a "stretch team," or team of people who will encourage and support you along your one-word journey. Our team became each other's stretch team. We celebrated our successes and sustained each other during our difficulties. Throughout the year, team members shared their one-word journeys. My team also encouraged their family members and friends to choose one word to guide their actions, and we enjoyed hearing about their journeys.

- Invite your family and friends to select one word that will be their driving force for the year.
- Encourage your team to invite their family and friends to select one word for the year.

CREATE YOUR ONE-WORD TEAM VISION

Your team can also select one word that will be the team vision for the year ahead. A vision is a declaration of what a group hopes to achieve and reflects the group's purpose. It represents the team's values, goals, and aspirations and becomes an active part of team discussions. To create a team vision, talk about what your team wants to achieve together. Brainstorm ideas and write them down. Try out a variety of words until you come up with a word that reflects your team's vision.

In 2019, our team selected the word *connect* as our one-word team vision. We wanted to collectively strive to connect with each other and to be more intentional with how we connected with the individuals whom we teach and coach. The next year, 2020, our one-word team vision was *evolve*. As a team, we wanted to evolve and pursue new avenues for training and coaching. Little did we know at that time how fitting that word would be. The COVID-19 pandemic forced us to evolve quickly as we converted all our training and coaching to a virtual platform. Our team was not satisfied to just use virtual platforms; they wanted to excel at making the experience joyful for participants. During team meetings, different members presented ideas on how to enhance the virtual learning experience through creative strategies.

Throughout the year, my team members were inspired to evolve in a variety of ways. We evolved through our team conversations and brainstorming sessions. Listening to the ideas and perspectives of others was an important part of our evolution. The process of evolving took time. Over several months, we examined how we wanted to evolve as a team. One goal was to become a more joyful team. During weekly meetings, we discussed topics related to joyful relationships, joyful workplace cultures, and joyful influence. We asked "What if . . ." questions to help us reimagine our work.

John Hittler (2018), in his article "The Genius of 'What If' Questions," says that this type of question can help your team imagine new possibilities. For example, if you were to ask them, "What if we evolved into a more joyful team? What would that look like?" you could begin to brainstorm possibilities. After brainstorming, turn the question into powerful declarations based on your discussion: "We will evolve into a more joyful team as we foster a joyful workplace culture." Begin to imagine what that would look like and how to make it happen. What would be different? What actions would we be taking?

Here is another example: What if we completely transformed our classroom or work environment to make it more joyful? What would it look like? What would it feel like?

What could we do to make our environment more joyful?

These are examples of the types of questions we discussed. Throughout the year, our team reimagined our interactions, our environments, and our work. We discussed tough topics and explored sensitive issues. We were able to tackle challenges creatively and think outside the box.

"You can either see yourself as a wave in the ocean, or you can see yourself as the ocean."

—**Oprah Winfrey** (attributed)

- Identify a "What if . . ." question to discuss with your team at your next meeting.
- Encourage your team to ask "What if . . ." questions related to their work.

"What if" questions can be a springboard to help start the flow of ideas. Thoughts built on thoughts, ideas built on ideas, and actions built on actions. As a leader, I took a step back and allowed my team to be bold and take some risks. I encouraged creativity and invited team members to perceive their work in new ways. As we embraced different perspectives, we made insightful discoveries. Our team discovered that their work was more joyful when they had opportunities to be creative. We found that creativity requires time and space.

One way to promote creative thought is to encourage team members to think of multiple ways to achieve the same outcome. Ask questions such as, "How else could we do it?" and "What else should be considered?" If you are the leader of a child-care center, you could ask your teachers to think creatively and brainstorm ideas for providing unique and meaningful learning experiences for the children. If you are the leader of your classroom, you could ask the children to share their ideas on how they would create a more joyful classroom. Creativity is cultivated with time and practice. As Maya Angelou said, "You can't use up creativity. The more you use, the more you have" (Elliot, 1989). Likewise, "What if" questions can help your team to think more creatively and reimagine their work.

Many of the ideas shared in this book are related to the implementation of the ideas from those brainstorming sessions. By continually focusing on our team's vision to *evolve*, we were motivated to take purposeful actions. These actions led to greater impacts within our team and community.

- Discuss with your team what they want to achieve together.

Invite your team to select one word that will be the team's driving force for the year.

Reimagining your purpose greatly influences how you think and act. We each have the potential for an impact as expansive as the ocean. Our view of who we are and what we can do is limited only by our thoughts. If I see myself as having the potential for a small wave of influence, that is most likely what my influence will be; however, if I envision myself with an ocean of influence, I begin to look at myself and what I can do differently. I have been transformed as a leader simply by reimagining my purpose. I now see myself as an ocean with larger, more expansive opportunities for elevating others and having a joyful influence on them. The joyful efforts of my team began as a wave that has expanded into an ocean of impact. You, too, can reimagine your purpose and yourself as a joyful leader, joyfully leading others.

DISCUSSION QUESTIONS

1. How can you reimagine your purpose?

2. What are some ways that you can win the moment?

3. What actions can you take to lighten your load?

4. What is one word that could be your driving force?

5. What if you had your team embark on one-word journeys? What might happen?

6. What benefits could your team gain by creating a one-word team vision?

REFLECTION ACTIVITY: NOW, WOW, POW, AND HOW

Think about the reading, and write down your thoughts for the following:

* **Now:** What is an idea or skill you can use right away?

  ____

  ____

  ____

* **Wow:** What is something that surprised you or that was new information?

  ____

  ____

  ____

* **Pow:** What is something that touched your heart or made an emotional connection?

  ____

  ____

  ____

* **How:** What is something you have questions about or would like to discuss?

  ____

  ____

  ____

ACTION PLAN

Determine one or more actions you will take this month to reimagine your purpose.

* Action:

___

___

___

* Why is this action important?

___

___

___

* What are my next steps?

___

___

___

CHAPTER 3

Radiate a Joyful Outlook

"Be a rainbow in somebody else's cloud."

—*Maya Angelou* (2014)

You rise as a joyful leader as you radiate a joyful outlook. Consider how you view the world. What do you spend your time thinking about? Thoughts are powerful and can influence how we see the world. If you allow negativity, fear, and doubt to take over your thoughts, they affect your personal and professional relationships. Likewise, if your thoughts focus on positivity and joy, this focus influences your interactions. As a leader, your outlook influences what you say and do. When you change your outlook, you subsequently change your words and actions. When you focus on joy and joyful interactions, your leadership changes in a positive and uplifting way. A joyful outlook is built on the premise that joy can be a part of every day. Being joyful becomes a conscious choice that requires individuals to be involved in taking time to look for joy, experience joy, and then savor the joyful moments.

Let's use the analogy of going to the eye doctor. When you go in for an eye exam, you are asked to read the eye chart down the rows of letters until you can no longer read them. If you are unable to read the letters and need glasses, the eye doctor has you look through a machine that helps to determine your prescription. The doctor asks you to look through different lenses and share whether you can see better with lens one or two. As the lens are flipped, your sight may be improved or diminished. Through a series of eliminations, the doctor determines the strength of the lenses you will need. This process takes time, but when the correct lens strength is selected, your view of the world is much clearer.

As leaders, sometimes we need corrective lenses. We may need to look through different lenses and remove the ones that are diminishing or negatively affecting our sight. We can instead select the lenses that will improve and enhance our outlook. When we view the world through these lenses, the world becomes a much clearer and happier place. In this chapter, we'll first look at how you, as a leader, can have a more joyful outlook and then share ways how you can cultivate a team that radiates a joyful outlook.

HOW TO HAVE A MORE JOYFUL OUTLOOK

To radiate a joyful outlook, leaders express gratitude and show appreciation, encourage others, foster a spirit of approval and acceptance, change their perspective and reframe their message, and verbalize positive affirmations. In this next section, we'll take an in-depth look into these qualities.

EXPRESSING GRATITUDE AND SHOWING APPRECIATION

Expressing gratitude is telling someone that you appreciate their efforts and thanking them for their contribution. Joyful leaders can express gratitude through both the spoken and written word. When was the last time you told someone thank you or sent a thank-you card, email, or text? It feels good to be appreciated and recognized through both spoken and written words. When we take time to notice the little things that others are doing for us, it also helps us feel more grateful.

One of the best ways to show appreciation is to tell a person what you appreciate about them. According to Gary Chapman and Paul White (2019), authors of *The 5 Languages of Appreciation in the Workplace: Empowering Organizations by Encouraging People*, people find value in different types of appreciation languages. Some languages have a deeper impact than others.

- **Words of affirmation:** Almost half (46 percent) of the workforce prefer receiving words that express appreciation for a job well done. These words should be specific and authentic.
- **Quality time:** Twenty-six percent of the workforce value receiving someone's undivided attention. They appreciated having someone listen to them and give them space for meaningful discussions.
- **Acts of service:** Twenty-two percent of the workforce appreciate small acts of service by co-workers. These acts of service include cleaning up after an event or taking on a work assignment when someone is overloaded with tasks.

- **Tangible gifts:** Six percent of the workforce prefer to receive thoughtful gifts that reflect the individual's interests.
- **Appropriate physical touch:** One percent of the workforce's appreciation language is physical touch, such as a high five, fist bump, or pat on the back.

Knowing your team's preferences can help you determine the most effective way to express appreciation.

In addition to leaders expressing gratitude and showing appreciation for their staff and colleagues, teachers can also show appreciation for the children in their classrooms by expressing gratitude and thanking them for their contributions. For example, thank children for being kind or throwing away their trash after lunch. Take time to listen to children's thoughts and ideas. Use appropriate physical touch. Do small acts of service that will bring joy to the receiver. When teachers consistently model appreciation and thankfulness, children will emulate their actions.

Write a letter of gratitude to a member of your team and read it to them aloud.

Invite all your team members to pair up, write a letter of appreciation to their partner, and share it with them.

Another way to express appreciation is by what leadership author, educator, and speaker Drew Dudley calls "lollipop moments." In his 2010 TED Talk "Everyday Leadership," he shared the following story. Just before Drew graduated from college, a young woman came up to him and told him that his actions four years earlier had greatly influenced her life. Drew said that he did not even remember her or the incident. The young woman shared that she was just about to start college when she met Drew. She was feeling overwhelmed and was ready to pack it in and go back home; however, she decided to go to a college event first. At the event, Drew was wearing a crazy hat and passing out lollipops to promote an organization. He came up to her and asked a young man standing next to her to give her a lollipop, which the young man shyly did. This simple interaction led to the young woman staying in college and spending a lot of time with the shy young man. (In fact, they were still together four years later and eventually were married.) The young lady thanked Drew for having a great influence on her life.

Because the incident included lollipops, Drew called it a "lollipop moment" or a moment in which someone says or does something that makes your life better. Drew began to think about people who had positively affected his life, and it changed his perspective on leadership. He began encouraging everyone to take time to thank and recognize the people who have positively influenced their lives.

I thought about individuals who had influenced my life, and I was inspired to write a thank-you note to Ingrid Fetell Lee, author of *Joyful: The Surprising Power of Ordinary Things to Create Extraordinary Happiness*. I expressed gratitude to her for the positive influence she had had on helping me become a more joyful leader, and I shared that she had also positive influenced the lives of the individuals I lead. I thanked her for helping me become a more joyful leader. Ingrid even wrote back and thanked me for my kind words.

I have also been the recipient of a lollipop moment. Denise was a director at a child-care center and an early childhood trainer who attended the Trainer Professional Learning Community (PLC) that I facilitate. She had an opportunity to apply for her dream job as an instructor at a community college. As part of the job interview, she needed to give a presentation to the department heads of the college. Denise told me that before she attended the Trainer PLC, she would have gone into her interview and given them a lecture about the requested topic. However, because of the things she had learned in the Trainer PLC, she developed an engaging and interactive presentation that included having the department heads get up and move to music. The presentation and interview went well. She was offered and accepted the job. One of the department heads later shared with her that her engaging presentation was one of the deciding factors in her being offered the job.

This was a wonderful and unexpected consequence of helping someone learn new skills. I was grateful she shared this lollipop moment with me.

- Share a lollipop moment with someone. Tell the person how they had a positive influence on your life.
- Challenge your team members to share a lollipop moment with someone.

"Anything that is of value in life only multiplies when it is given."

—Deepak Chopra (1994)

ENCOURAGING OTHERS

To encourage is to lift others up. Joyful leaders inspire, cheer others on, and focus on what is working rather than discouraging individuals from even trying. They encourage others when they express excitement and joy about their ideas.

This happened with Nikki, one of my team members who is passionate about self-care. Noticing her interest in self-care, I encouraged her to incorporate some of those ideas into her work. She was excited to give teachers ideas on how to implement daily self-care habits. During one of her training sessions, Nikki gave each teacher a box and told them to take their boxes home and create a "You Matter" box. She invited them to decorate their boxes and write a message to themselves about how they matter to families in their program, then to place their messages in their boxes. Nikki encouraged the teachers to bring their "You Matter" boxes to work and put them in the staff lounge along with an invitation for other staff members to write notes expressing why the teacher matters to the children and families in their program. The teachers felt uplifted, and several of them went one step further and created a "You Matter" box for Nikki. They wrote messages thanking her for encouraging them. They were grateful for the positive ways she had influenced them to be more mindful of their self-care and outlook. This is an example of how encouraging others can lead to a more joyful outlook for both the giver and the receiver.

"Diversity is being invited to the party; inclusion is being asked to dance."

—Vernā Myers, diversity advocate and speaker

FOSTERING A SPIRIT OF ACCEPTANCE AND APPROVAL

Fostering a spirit of acceptance and approval happens when we value what others have to say and we include them by asking them to be part of the conversation. Joyful leaders avoid criticizing others; they are accepting and respectfully listen and learn. When team members feel accepted for who they are and what they think, they are more likely to engage in positive interactions. This does not mean that everyone must agree with everyone's ideas, but there should be a spirit of acceptance and approval for ideas that are different from your own (and among your team members). Teams with a spirit of acceptance and approval establish an environment that embraces diverse viewpoints, where they intentionally listen to each person's point of view respectfully. Likewise, by modeling this strategy, children will learn how to be open to new ideas and perspectives.

Think of your team as a beautiful mosaic, a picture produced by arranging many small, colored pieces of tile or glass together. Each tile has a beauty of its own, yet when the tiles are carefully selected and arranged, the mosaic is striking. To ensure that the beauty of the mosaic is maintained, each tile must be carefully polished. Likewise, as a leader, you can help keep each person's skills polished through mentoring and coaching. Instead of pointing out smudges, spots, and blemishes, help your team members gain a greater appreciation for their unique contributions to the group. As a leader, be open and appreciative in accepting the feedback you receive from the individuals you lead. Be thoughtful and reflective. Continue to "polish their tiles" by supporting their efforts. These actions will foster a spirit of acceptance and approval.

As a leader, you can also give team members opportunities to learn more about each other's beliefs and preferences. Set an example of how to acknowledge differences and respectfully respond to conflicting ideas. You could say, for example, "Thank you for sharing your ideas. I want to understand your perspective. Can you tell me more?"

"It appears we have different opinions on the subject. Let's look deeper and see if we can find some common ground. Can we talk more about the topic next week?"

It often helps if you take time to think before you speak. Sometimes silence is the best response.

"The smallest change in perspective can transform a life. What tiny attitude adjustment might turn your world around?"

—**Oprah Winfrey** (attributed)

Be intentional and invite everyone to respond and participate. Model using respectful language and thank individuals for sharing their thoughts and ideas. Ask for more information to ensure you truly understand what the other person is saying. Express care and concern for each person. Let them know that you value their contribution to the team.

- Engage in behaviors that foster a spirit of acceptance and approval.
- Invite your team to engage in behaviors that foster a spirit of acceptance and approval.

CHANGING YOUR PERSPECTIVE AND REFRAMING YOUR MESSAGE

Our outlook is influenced by how we perceive different aspects of our lives. Changing your perspective or how you view your circumstances can influence how you view the world. Joyful leaders seek to see the positive aspects of a situation. That does not mean that you look at everything through rose-colored glasses. When things are not going well, it is okay to be open and honest about the challenges. Recognize what you do, and do not, have control over. Sometimes, simply changing your perspective or reframing your message can provide the active hope that is needed to face the challenge.

Reflect for a moment about your thoughts. Are your thoughts more negative or positive? Which thoughts are causing you stress? Thoughts are powerful and can affect how you feel and how you act. One way to change your thoughts is by reframing your message. For example, by changing the words you use to describe a situation, obstacles become opportunities and setbacks become different paths to follow.

You can flip the script of your thought patterns by changing a negative thought into a positive thought. If I fail at something and think to myself, "I'm a failure. I can't do anything right," I'll try to change my thoughts—flip the script—to something like "I'm learning and growing. With time and effort, I'll get it."

- Flip the script. Redefine challenges and difficulties that you are facing by reframing your message. Change negative words to positive phrases. Does your perspective change if you redefine your challenges and difficulties as learning opportunities?

- Invite your team to reframe their messages and guide them on how to change the negative words to positive phrases.

We may not understand the perspectives of others until we ask for clarification. If someone says or does something hurtful, instead of immediately expressing anger and resentment, reframe the situation and seek further clarification. This can help lower your stress level and act as a buffer, preventing your strong emotions from overcoming your being. Seek greater understanding. Remember, everyone has a story, so when you can, take time to listen and learn.

VERBALIZING POSITIVE AFFIRMATIONS

"Focus on the four things you can control in your life: what you think, what you say, what you feel, and what you do."

—Gordon and West (2019)

Another way to radiate a more joyful outlook is by verbalizing positive and joyful affirmations. Affirmations are phrases that you say to reinforce your ideas and beliefs. Speaking joyful affirmations can help you focus on the positive and joyful aspects of your life and set the tone for your day. Using self-affirmations has been shown to decrease stress and increase resilience, which can lead to positive changes in behavior (Cohen and Sherman, 2014). Here is an example of some heartfelt and joyful affirmations that I use to begin my day. You are encouraged to try saying these affirmations aloud and then create your own positive affirmations, personalized to your ideas and beliefs.

* Joy begins with me.
* I will choose to be joyful each day.
* I will notice joyful moments.
* I will savor joyful moments.
* I see joy. Joy is all around me.
* I am joyful. I feel and give joy.
* Joy radiates from my being.
* Today will be joyful.
* Joy begins with me.

When I affirm that I am joyful, I feel more joyful, and I begin to think of ways to add joy to my day.

Now that we have explored five ways you can radiate a more joyful outlook, let's look at some ways that you can lead a more joyful and effective team.

HOW TO LEAD A MORE JOYFUL AND EFFECTIVE TEAM

Once you have strengthened your outlook, you can focus on creating a joyful and effective team. Teams that are more joyful have been found to be more effective. Researchers Oswald, Proto, and Sgroi (2015) determined that happier workers were 10 percent to 12 percent more productive. By creating a more joyful team, you will also be creating a more effective and productive team.

"Joy, collected over time, fuels resilience—ensuring we'll have reservoirs of emotional strength when hard things do happen."

—Brené Brown (2013b)

Think about the individuals you lead or the children you teach. What is working? Not working?

A few years ago, I considered my team in that context. Overall, my team was productive and supportive of each other, but they were primarily working independently. They didn't have many opportunities to work collaboratively on projects. Sometimes, I felt that everyone was just going through the motions and getting things done, but we had lost our spark. We needed something to reignite and reinvigorate our team—opportunities to be creative, strengthen our relationships, and bring more joy into our work.

An opportunity presented itself. My team came together to plan the first Early Childhood Trainer conference in our state. Everyone was encouraged to be creative and think outside the box. We created a safe environment that encouraged divergent thinking and collaborative work. The most significant outcome was that we became a more joyful and effective team.

To successfully lead a joyful and effective team, a leader must:

* create an emotionally safe environment,
* cultivate the team,
* focus on each member's strengths, and
* be openly optimistic.

CREATE AN EMOTIONALLY SAFE ENVIRONMENT

Staff must first feel emotionally safe within the team. Researchers at Google (re:Work, n.d.) conducted extensive research (Project Aristotle) to discover the main factors that would help leaders create the perfect team. The Google researchers thought that building the finest teams would require bringing the best people together. Surprisingly, the researchers found that the "who" part of the equation was less important than the "how." Teams were more successful when members showed sensitivity and listened to one another. They found that if a team member shares an idea that is important to them, and that idea is ignored or dismissed, the team member may feel invalidated. That can have a negative impact not only on the individual but also on the team. Some other factors that were important to team effectiveness included the following:

* Dependability: Getting things done on time and completing quality work
* Structure and Clarity: Having clear job expectations, roles, plans, and goals
* Meaning: Finding a sense of purpose or importance in the work
* Impact: Belief that the work matters and the team's efforts are making a difference

Google determined that psychological safety or a shared belief that the team was safe for interpersonal risk-taking was the most important factor in building effective teams. Individuals with higher levels of psychological safety were also less likely to leave an organization. I found this research fascinating: an effective team is less about who is on the team and more on how members interact with one another.

This can also be true in early childhood classrooms. To create a cohesive and effective early childhood classroom, the children need to feel emotionally safe to share their thoughts and feelings.

Researchers determined that psychological safety or a shared belief that the team was safe for interpersonal risk-taking was the most important factor in building effective teams.

> One child in Ms. Isabel's preschool class had lost his father in a car accident. It was a very sad and emotional time for the child and the family. The child did not come to class for a couple of weeks, and the children were asking about their friend. With the family's permission, Isabel shared with her class that the child had lost one of his parents. She told them that their friend was sad and asked them if they would like to draw some pictures to give to him. The children drew pictures, and the class wrote a letter telling their friend that they missed him and hoped he would feel better soon. Isabel kept in contact with the family, and they discussed how they could best support the child when he returned to class.
>
> A few days before the child returned to class, his mother asked if he could share some pictures and memories of his dad when he returned. Isabel agreed. She shared with her class that their friend would be returning to class in a few days and would be sharing some special memories he had with his dad. She told the children that he would need their friendship and kindness. She shared some ways they could be a caring friend. When he returned to class, the children welcomed him back and listened as he shared his memories of his dad. The class was kind and understanding when he was sad or needed some time alone. They created an emotionally safe classroom for their friend who was grieving the loss of his father.

In this example, Isabel helped her students model an emotionally safe environment where the child who lost his father felt comfortable sharing his thoughts and feelings.

- Write down one new way that you can create an emotionally safe climate within your team or classroom.
- Discuss with your team how you can work together to create an emotionally safe climate.

CULTIVATE THE TEAM

The most productive and cohesive teams combine individual drive with the power of teamwork. Team members work to connect, inspire each other, and engage in meaningful activities. Cultivating joyful and effective teams does not happen overnight; it is a process that takes place one step at a time. It is important to be realistic and optimistic about what can happen over time. Leaders may find some team members are in different places in their thinking, and ongoing, intentional actions may be needed to create the foundation for your team's transformation. When leaders are authentic, honest, and lead by example, they exemplify the actions that they want to promote.

It might be helpful to think about the different stages that teams go through. In 1965, Bruce W. Tuckman, an educational psychologist and researcher, proposed a four-stage model of effective group formation (Bonebright, 2010; Wilson, n.d.).

This model is widely recognized for describing team dynamics and the stages of growth within developing teams. The four-stage model of team development includes:

- **Forming:** Team members are coming together and learning about each other.
- **Storming:** Teams are encountering different types of conflict and disagreements. Teams are working through issues and learning to accept issues and overcome obstacles.
- **Norming:** Teams are able to resolve issues and are establishing team goals.
- **Performing:** Teams are working together cooperatively and are focused on solving problems and moving forward to meet team goals.

Tuckman later added a fifth stage, adjourning, to describe the end of a team project.

Teams can go back and forth between the different stages. For example, a few years ago, my team was in the stage of performing. Team members actively demonstrated mutual respect, collaboration, and effective communication. They worked together to meet team goals. Then, we had a new member join our team, temporarily disrupting the team dynamics. We moved back to the stage of forming. The new team member needed time to feel emotionally safe, and we needed time to feel comfortable with her. Some issues needed to be resolved. The new team member also needed time to acclimate into our team culture. After a few months, she became an integral part of our team. We moved through the stages of storming and norming and then returned to the stage of performing as everyone was able to develop trusting relationships and psychological safety with each other.

Early childhood classrooms go through similar stages as children come together and learn from each other. When a new child or new teacher enters the classroom, there is a period of adjustment. Time is needed for everyone to feel emotionally safe with each other, as Marietta discovered when she moved into teaching in the toddler room.

> Becoming a teacher in the toddler room was an adjustment for both Marietta and the children. She had been in the preschool classroom, so moving to a younger age group was a big change for her. She loved the toddlers' enthusiasm and energy, but sometimes her expectations did not align with the young children's abilities or temperaments. Several of the toddlers were not responding to her attempts to form a relationship and would burst into tears when she entered the room. Marietta talked to the other teachers and her director about her situation. They helped her develop some strategies to try and encouraged her to be patient. It takes time to build trust and develop relationships. Within a few weeks, Marietta became more comfortable with the children, and they were responding positively to her care and attention. She was building a relationship with each child and had adjusted her expectations to match the needs of toddlers. The children were feeling safe and secure in her presence.

FOCUS ON EACH MEMBER'S STRENGTHS

Joyful leaders and team members focus on strengths and look for the good in others. They are encouraging and supportive. As you cultivate a joyful and effective team, think about the characteristics of joyful team members. What would they say and do? Sometimes it is helpful to give team members specific roles within your team. Here are some examples:

- **Morale Booster:** enthusiastically promotes confidence and hopefulness within the team
- **Sounding Board:** listens to problems and ideas, gives objective insights
- **Encourager:** gives other team members smiles, friendly greetings, and words of encouragement
- **Guide:** offers suggestions when team members are feeling stuck and need help with tasks
- **Listener:** listens to what others have to say
- **Helping Hand:** jumps in and helps team members as needed
- **Courageous Person:** gives others courage during difficulties
- **Empathetic Person:** welcomes the ideas and opinions of others, takes time to view situations from the other person's perspective
- **Creative Inspiration:** offers imaginative and original ideas
- **Fun Maker:** adds an element of fun to team meetings and events

How would these roles or similar types of roles benefit your team? What would happen if you invited children in your classroom to take on some of these roles?

Think about your team and the different roles they could take on to be joyful team members.

Discuss different roles team members can take within a joyful team. Invite the individuals you lead to take on one or more of the roles.

BE OPENLY OPTIMISTIC

Leaders and teams that are openly optimistic expect the best outcomes and are inspired and motivated to work toward their shared vision. They believe that things will turn out favorably. Openly optimistic teams view problems as issues that need to be solved. They look for the best in each situation and work together to overcome concerns as they arise. Challenges are seen as temporary setbacks, not as permanent obstructions.

"Part of being optimistic is keeping one's head pointed toward the sun, one's feet moving forward."

—Nelson Mandela (2007)

To be openly optimistic, team members notice actions, words, and deeds that are positive and uplifting. For example, one of our joyful team members greets everyone with a smile and encouraging words. She is willing to help with whatever tasks need to be accomplished. This sets the tone for team interactions. Her positive energy ripples to other team members, who in turn share their positive energy with others.

Using a strengths-based lens during interactions is another way to work toward being openly optimistic. A strengths-based lens focuses on individuals' positive attributes and actions and assumes everyone has unique characteristics and their own story.

Openly optimistic individuals look for the positive aspects of life and work. They are willing to work through challenges and know they have the power to overcome them. They seek and strive to connect emotionally with others. To be optimistic includes focusing on your strengths and the strengths of others. It also means giving yourself grace when things do not go as expected. Openly optimistic individuals spend time doing activities they enjoy and practice healthy self-care habits. They imagine a positive future for themselves and the individuals they lead.

- Determine one way you can lead your team to be openly optimistic. Then, act on it.
- Discuss with your team how they can be openly optimistic with each other and the people they serve, then encourage them to act.

DISCUSSION QUESTIONS

1. What actions can you take to radiate a more joyful outlook?

2. How can you express gratitude and appreciation to others?

3. What are some ways you can encourage the individuals you lead?

4. What behaviors foster a spirit of acceptance and approval within your team or classroom?

5. How could you reframe your message?

6. What are some positive affirmations you could say to yourself?

7. What characteristics of a joyful and effective team does your team exhibit? What characteristics could your team develop to become more joyful and effective?

REFLECTION ACTIVITY: IOU

- Insights: What are several insights that you gained from the reading?

- Opportunities: What opportunities are there for you to incorporate what you learned from the reading into your professional practices?

- Unique or Useful Ideas: What ideas from the reading did you find to be unique or useful?

ACTION PLAN

Determine one or more actions you will take this month to radiate a joyful outlook.

- Action:

  ___

  ___

  ___

- Why is this action important?

  ___

  ___

  ___

- What are my next steps?

  ___

  ___

  ___

CHAPTER 4

Engage in Joyful Actions

"She found Joy and Wonder in every little thing. And Joy and Wonder always found her."

—Katrina Mayer

You rise as a leader by engaging in joyful actions. I would describe my actions as joyful when I feel upbeat, festive, lighthearted, or even jubilant while doing them. The following are some examples of how early childhood teachers and leaders describe actions that are joyful:

* "I love when children enthusiastically share with their parents what they did that day in my classroom."
* "Giggles! Children's smiles and excitement."

* "The light-bulb moments when my team discovers new thoughts and ideas."
* "The pure joy and excitement children have when they accomplish something."

Joyful actions often happen when adults and children have opportunities to be creative. These actions can be as simple as a smile or sharing a laugh together. Joy is found when kindness is shared, and individuals feel hopeful. Not all actions as a leader will be joyful, but many leadership actions can become more joyful by focusing on the difference your leadership is having on others.

This chapter discusses how you as a leader can engage your team in joyful actions by inviting and involving them in establishing a workplace culture that supports these actions. According to Kegan and Lahey (2016), authors of *An Everyone Culture*, "Research shows that the single biggest cause of work burnout is not work overload but working too long without experiencing your own personal development." Focusing on the personal development of your team members is an important aspect of developing a joyful workplace culture. Let's start at the beginning: getting your team on board.

INVITE TEAM MEMBERS ON A JOYFUL JOURNEY

A few years ago, I invited my team members to go on a joyful journey with me. I explained that this would be an ongoing endeavor, and we would travel it together. During our journey, we would be talking about joy, participating in joyful activities, and establishing a joyful workplace culture. I shared that I wasn't sure what the journey would look like, but I hoped it would transform our work and interactions. It was up to our team to determine what the journey would include and what actions we would take together. As we embarked, we brainstormed and talked about the expectations, behaviors, and characteristics of joyful teams. When I asked my team members to share their description of a joyful team, one person shared, "Joyful teams are positive. The energy of the team is optimistic, hopeful, and motivating. The mindset of the team is focused on what is possible and not on what is impossible." As leaders of joyful teams, it is important to focus on what is possible.

My team also discussed the types of actions that a joyful team would take. Team members shared that it would be important to encourage and support each other during the journey. They thought it would be great if there were more opportunities to develop and share their talents and interests with each other. My team wanted to have fun together and collaborate on creative projects. They hoped they would form closer connections with each other and joyfully influence the individuals they teach. They looked forward to engaging in joyful actions together.

My team's journey started several years ago. It took time and a concerted effort to build a joyful team culture. Initially, our team spent a lot of time talking about joy and how to have joyful interactions and establish a joyful culture. Over time, team conversations became less frequent, but joy was still an integral part of our workplace culture. I will often hear team members talking to each other about their joyspotting. They also like to share joyful experience that they have had with the individuals they teach.

Remember, the journey is more important than the destination. You will learn and grow as you go down the path together. Here are some things we learned during our journey.

PERSEVERE DURING THE TOUGH TIMES

Some days, it is hard to feel joyful. When individuals are going through tough situations, it can be much harder to find joy in circumstances. We sometimes become rigid in our thinking and have a harder time considering alternatives. To help individuals with fixed thinking, psychologist Marsha Linehan (2014) pioneered dialectical behavioral therapy, which guides individuals to understand that opposite ideas can both be true at the same time. A simpler way to understand this concept is by using "The & Principle," as shared by educational consultant Arianna Howard (2020). The & Principle gives individuals permission to feel more than one emotion at a time. For example, on the first day of school, I can feel nervous *and* excited. A person can feel sorrow *and* gratitude or distress *and* joy. Understanding The & Principle gave our team permission to feel conflicting emotions and reminded us that we could feel joy even when facing life's challenges. The & Principle let us to be more intentional in finding joy in the little things. When I wasn't feeling very joyful, I took a moment to focus on things that I was grateful for, such as my family and health. I would look at pictures of my children and grandchildren and think about joyful times we had spent together. For a few brief moments, I felt a sense of joy and thankfulness. These moments renewed my hope in having better days ahead. It can also be helpful to share your difficulties with individuals you trust. When my joy bucket is low, I seek others who can help me fill my bucket.

LAUGH AND HAVE FUN TOGETHER

Laughter changes your mental health to a more positive and joyful state of mind. There are many therapeutic benefits of laughter therapy according to researcher JongEun Yim (2016). Laughter has been shown to decrease stress and improve your quality of life. Smiling and laughing are contagious and can boost your immune system by releasing endorphins that help you feel more positive. One of my team's favorite things to do is to have brainstorming sessions related to work projects. We encourage creativity during these sessions, and welcome all ideas, no matter how outlandish they may seem because we know that ideas build on ideas. We do not take ourselves too seriously. Likewise, we find the humor in our humanness and let go of stress as we laugh at our mistakes and move on. Together, we are building joyful memories that will sustain us when we are struggling or facing a challenge.

KNOW—AND EXPECT—THAT THINGS OFTEN WILL NOT GO AS PLANNED

With joy as our focus, we talk about problems as challenging opportunities that we will overcome together. We have learned to accept situations for what they are and work to improve them the best way we can. For example, when we converted all our training to a virtual format during the pandemic, we quickly learned that when technology is involved, things often do not go as planned. As a team, we discussed strategies and developed plans for what to do when the unexpected happens. One of our best plans was to find humor in the situation and then do our best to quickly resolve the issue. When we faced a technological challenge, we involved learners in the process and invited them to have patience with technology. This set the tone for more joyful and less stressful training sessions for us and our learners.

One thing that really shaped our experience was that we were committed to go on the journey together. We found more joy in our work and personal lives within a supportive environment. We noticed a difference in our interactions and in our work. Team members liked coming to work because it was a happy place to be. An unanticipated outcome was that the positivity of our team members rippled to coworkers, students, and community partners. Others noticed a difference in how we interacted, and they were curious about what helped our team get along so well and work together in such a productive manner. The secret ingredient was joy.

Remember, talking about something repeatedly gives it importance. Talking about joy made it a part of our team culture. During your journey, encourage everyone to develop their abilities to find joy, create joy, feel joy, and share joyful energy.

- Invite your team to join you on a joyful journey.
- Encourage your team to brainstorm and identify expectations, behaviors, and characteristics of joyful teams.

INVOLVE ALL TEAM MEMBERS IN JOYFUL ACTIONS

One of the key elements of a successful joyful journey is to involve everyone. Team members will have more buy-in if they are an integral part of the process. Invite team members to take the lead on engaging in different joyful activities and experiences. Do not try to do everything yourself, as that is a quick road to burnout. Joyful leaders trust their team and rejoice in their abilities. Give your team members opportunities to blossom with creativity. Many leaders may feel that they don't have time for these types of nonwork-related activities. I have found that when you take a few minutes to focus on joy, the overall productivity of your team goes up. Team members actually get more done throughout the day because they feel joyful and are ready to meet the challenges of the day.

Not all joyful activities need to take place during work hours. Engage in joyful actions outside of work. For example, hold a barbecue and games in a local park for your team and their families and pets. Encourage team members to take walks and eat lunch together. Create a Joy Blast Board where team members can share photos of joyful moments. What's important is to give your team opportunities to participate in joyful actions. The best ideas will be the ones that your team members come up with and take the lead on implementing. All you need to do is to create the foundation and let your team take it from there.

Let's look at several ideas to involve your team in joyful actions by encouraging a sense of playfulness, promoting creativity, adding joyful beginnings to your team meetings, engaging in selfless service, lifting each other up, and celebrating together to pave the way for cultivating a joyful workplace culture.

ENCOURAGE A SENSE OF PLAYFULNESS

Young children naturally know how to be playful. They know how to have fun, be open to the moment, embrace a surprise, do something delightful, and enjoy new experiences. As a leader, you can encourage your team to reconnect with this sense of playfulness.

Giant Jenga is one playful activity that we used to help get to know each other. Jenga is a game in which players stack wooden blocks into a tower and then take turns removing one block at a time, hoping they will not cause the tower to come tumbling down. For our game, we added colored stickers to each block. After removing a block, a team member drew from a jar a getting-to-know-you question on a piece of paper that matched the color of the sticker. Questions included, "What inspires you?" and "What is one thing on your bucket list?" Team members had fun supporting each other as they attempted to remove the Jenga blocks and got to know everyone better.

Adults often become more playful when they try new things and experience the unexpected. Kathleen Alfano (n.d.), a child development and play expert and former director of research at Fisher-Price, says it best: "Play empowers people to be flexible thinkers, creative, young-at-heart and free spirited. It provides an opportunity for pure enjoyment." Playing Giant Jenga was pure enjoyment. We laughed together, felt young at heart, and increased our ability as a team to be flexible and creative thinkers. Play can be an important part of the work you do because it will open the mind to new and innovative possibilities.

Another playful thing that we did as a team was to participate in an escape room. It was a great experience to work together in an unusual way. There was such a fun element of playfulness as we searched for clues and worked together to escape from the room. Team members approached the task using their personal strengths; some team members worked independently, and others partnered up to find clues and unlock the mysteries of the room. By building on each other's ideas, our team had the successful outcome of escaping the room in less than one hour. We left the event invigorated and ready to face new challenges together.

Following the activity, we debriefed and discussed how we could use our escape-room skills in our work. There were some "Aha!" moments as team members realized how they had worked together and also independently to solve the clues. One team member commented on how she had seen different members use specific strengths, such as solving picture puzzles and reading maps. Our team became more aware of the benefits of working collaboratively toward a unified goal. We had a greater appreciation for how team members had used innovative ideas and persistence in getting the job done in a timely manner. We discussed how we could use these skills in our work. Playfulness had made a difference in our ability to work collaboratively.

Catherine Price, author of *The Power of Fun: How to Feel Alive Again* (2021) said, "What we don't realize is that, far from being frivolous or selfish, the pursuit of fun will help us achieve all of these goals. Life is not a zero-sum equation: we can care about fun and be conscientious citizens who are committed to improving the world—indeed fun can give us more energy with which to do so. And if we want our own lives to be satisfying and joyful, true fun isn't optional. It shouldn't be an afterthought. It should be our guiding star." I hope you will allow playfulness and fun to be your guiding star.

- Plan one way your team can engage together in joyful playfulness.
- Engage in joyful playfulness with your team.

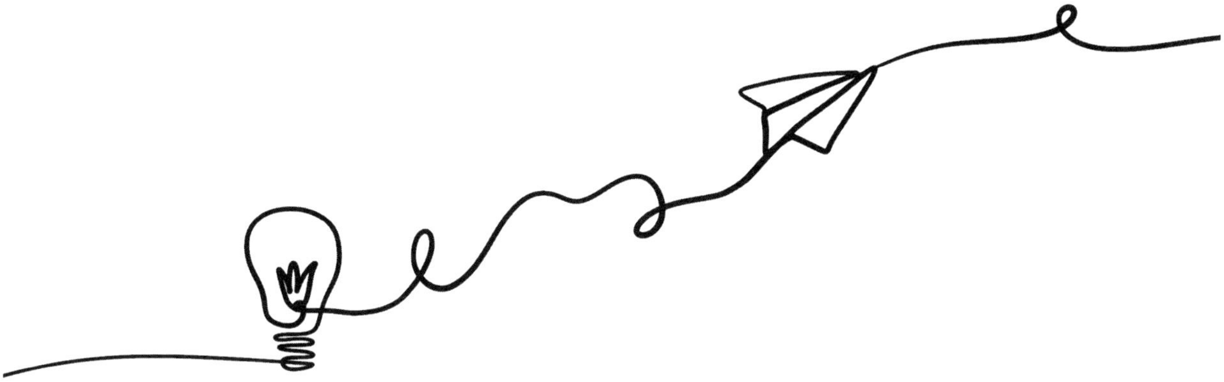

PROMOTE CREATIVITY

Taking time for playfulness can help with creativity. Being creative is more than imagining ideas; it is also the act of bringing those ideas to life. In her article "What Is Creativity? (And Why Is It a Crucial Factor for Business Success?)" Linda Naiman (2021) states, "Creativity is the act of turning new and imaginative ideas into reality. Creativity is characterized by the ability to perceive the world in new ways, to find hidden patterns, to make connections between seemingly unrelated phenomena, and to generate solutions." Often, creativity results in engaging in joyful actions. Let me share one way our team engaged in a project that required lots of creativity and joyful actions:

> After the pandemic began to ease up and our team was able to meet in person again, we discussed how we could rejuvenate our passion and creativity. The idea that generated the most enthusiasm was to hold the first conference in Nevada for early childhood trainers. Our team wanted to create an experience that trainers would remember, while enhancing their skills as trainers. We wanted to provide trainers with ideas on how to be creative and effective in offering professional learning to the early childhood community.
>
> The theme we selected for the trainer conference was "Your Destination for T.O.P. Training Techniques." (TOP was an acronym for themes, objects, and props.) Throughout the conference, my team modeled how trainers could enhance learning by using themes, objects, and props. Each conference session featured a unique theme for the training environment. For example, Wonders of the World featured international flags and posters of sites from around the world. During check-in, each attendee received their boarding pass (personal conference itinerary) and a passport. Trainers received destination stickers to add to their passports as they attended different sessions.

Teresa's Treasure Island was the trainers' first destination. There, trainers discovered treasures and gems designed to enhance their ability to be effective and engaging facilitators of professional learning. Trainers were invited to earn gems throughout the conference and bedazzle a card with them. They earned the New Friend Gem for meeting new people and earned the Aha Gem for having an "Aha!" moment during the conference. Trainers also went on a treasure hunt and solved clues. For the last clue, they opened a small treasure chest and found a colorful gem. They were invited to find someone with the same color jewel and share a "gem" that they had learned and wanted to implement.

In the afternoon, trainers took an excursion to Fidget Island where they received a fidget and visited seven smaller islands. Each island featured a hands-on training technique such as using sticky-note polls or playing playdough charades. The purpose of this destination was to demonstrate that short lessons on specific strategies can be a powerful way to train adult learners. When trainers arrived the second day of the conference, they traveled to Viva Las Vegas and learned how to implement Energizers with Pizzazz. Later, they took a pretend cruise in a training room set up to look like an ocean liner and discovered environments that inspire. Everyone was quite surprised when Russell, the little boy from the movie *Up*, arrived with his balloons and taught trainers how they could soar with presentations that pop.

After lunch, trainers returned to Teresa's Treasure Island to take five minutes to reflect and respond to four specific questions. They were then invited to connect and reflect within small groups, which we called Care Circles. Within the Care Circles, the trainers shared their responses to the four reflection questions. Trainers shared the gems they had gained throughout the conference and the strategies that they were going to treasure and implement in future training sessions. The conference concluded with a slide show featuring photos from the two-day event, and then we took a photo of everyone in the flower garden to capture a joyful memory.

The conference was a labor of love. My team went above and beyond to make it an unforgettable experience. They felt great joy, and the attendees expressed their happiness at being part of the event. This creative, collaborative effort rejuvenated my team's passion for training adult learners joyfully.

Promoting creativity as a way to engage in joyful actions can also happen in the early childhood classroom:

Mr. Bernardo sought to create a welcoming environment within his classroom that reflected his heritage. He involved the preschoolers in creating an Italian village. They looked at photos, watched videos, and brainstormed ideas. Together they developed a design for their village that included a "brick" wall that the children created out of painted cardboard trays. They set up tables and chairs to create a cozy restaurant that featured twinkly lights and hanging plants. Small groups of children created different shops, including a farmer's market where goods and services could be exchanged. The children were eager to share their village with their families and planned a family event. They made invitations and other preparations, and then they welcomed the families into the joyful environment and invited them to take a tour of the village. At each stop, small groups of children would talk about their shop and how they had created it. The tour ended with a celebration of food and friendship.

Think about how you could promote creativity in your classroom or program. Consider using these steps:

* Brainstorm ideas with your team.
* Select an idea that energizes your team.
* Work together on the idea.
* Be open to innovative thoughts and actions.
* Bring the idea to life.
* Celebrate your creativity!

INCLUDE JOYFUL BEGINNINGS

In addition to promoting creativity, play can also strengthen your team's ability to work together collaboratively. As mentioned earlier, during the pandemic, our team had to quickly convert all our training and coaching to a virtual learning format. This process was challenging, stressful, time-consuming, and at times, a real joy zapper. I contemplated how I could best support and help my team find joy in the chaos. During one of our team meetings, we brainstormed ideas on how to be more playful as a team, because play can be a great stress buster. One idea was to start each of our team meetings with a "Joyful Beginning," which would last about five to ten minutes and add an element of fun to the beginning of our meetings. By investing a few minutes on a joyful beginning to our meeting, we discovered that the remaining meeting time became much more productive. We took turns facilitating a joyful beginning at the start of our team meetings. Appendix D lists fifty-two joyful beginnings, one for each week of the year. Here are just a few that have been particularly successful for our team:

* **Joyful Scavenger Hunt:** One week prior to the team meeting, invite everyone to participate in a joyful scavenger hunt. Give each team member a list (see appendix B), and ask them find different kinds of joyful items and list what they found. At the team meeting, have each team member share one or more of the joyful items they found.
* **Guess Who?** Ask each team member to submit a baby or childhood picture, and then have one team member create a slideshow. Encourage team members to guess whose baby picture is whose. Our team members also created a slide presentation that featured the place where each team member was born and some of their childhood memories. Team members made connections as they learned more about where everyone had grown up, from Pittsburgh to El Paso, from Cleveland to Oakland.
* **Zoom around the Room:** Inspired by a game played on *The Kelly Clarkson Show*, ask team members to find something in a particular category (for example, something yellow). Give everyone one minute to zoom around the room and find something in that category. You'll be amazed at the variety of items team members find. Some other ideas for categories include finding something joyful, something round, or something playful.

- **Fill the Joy Jar:** Invite team members to write down quotes, inspirational messages, and joyful ideas on strips of colorful paper and place them in a jar called the Joy Jar. Before a meeting, ask a few people to share their quotes or inspirational messages. Encourage team members to continue to add messages to the Joy Jar and take out a strip of paper and read a message whenever they needed a little extra joy in their day.
- **Joyful Bingo:** A week before the meeting, give everyone a Bingo card (see an example in appendix C). Invite everyone to mark off items until they mark off five items in a row and have Bingo. Items could include watching a sunset, wrapping yourself in a soft warm blanket, savoring a favorite food, or listening to some beautiful music. Include several "your choice" boxes so that everyone has an opportunity to create their own personal joyful experience. Invite team members to share several of the items they have crossed off their Bingo cards.

ENGAGE IN SELFLESS SERVICE

Encourage your team to engage in selfless service by giving of their time and talents to others. Helping someone else can be a joyful action that can be uplifting for both the receiver and the giver.

When someone on our team was having health issues or another challenge, team members provided selfless service by stepping in and teaching a class or completing a project. They acted without any expectation of reciprocity. An atmosphere of selfless service is built when leaders engage in service as well. As a team, we have taken opportunities to clean books; fill backpacks for children in foster care; and collect food, clothing, and other items for local organizations. These have been joyful experiences that have brought us closer as a team. We can also learn about kindness by watching the actions of young children.

> Three-year-old Miranda was playing outside when she noticed that her friend Lizzie was crying. She went over and put her arm around Lizzie's shoulder and ask what was wrong. Lizzie said she had lost Rumby, her stuffed rabbit. Miranda said she would go find it, and she raced around looking for Rumby. She asked other children to help in the search. Everyone started looking for Rumby. Miranda was so excited when she found Rumby in a basket under some other toys that she rushed over to Lizzie, holding out Rumby. Lizzie's face lit up, and she joyfully hugged her beloved toy. Then, she hugged Miranda and the two girls grinned from ear to ear and went off to play. It was a small and simple act of kindness that joyfully influenced both girls.

Another way to engage is selfless service is through random acts of kindness. Have you ever pulled up to the drive-through and discovered the person in front of you had already paid for your meal? That simple act makes your day seem brighter and more joyful. You may even want to pay it forward and show kindness to others. We often feel joyful when we are kind to others. In fact, joyful actions can build your resilience and contribute to having a surplus of joy!

A few years ago, I was at a professional conference with a friend. We saw an older woman standing by a table, looking concerned. We went over to talk to her. She told us that she was with her daughter, and she did not know where her daughter had gone. We reassured her that her daughter was probably just getting her some food and would be back soon. My friend and I continued to reassure her. Within a few minutes, her daughter came back with two plates of food. She thanked us for taking time to talk to her mom, as she is often anxious in unfamiliar settings. She appreciated us helping to keep her mom calm until she returned. It was a little thing and yet it really brightened my day. It reminded me how small acts of kindness can make a big difference to someone else.

- Do a random act of kindness.
- Encourage your team members to do acts of kindness for each other.

LIFT EACH OTHER UP

When we lift others, we are also uplifted. Engaging in joyful actions as a team includes finding ways to lift others, especially when they are going through hard times. One of our team members was going through a difficult time after losing several loved ones within a short period. As a team, we wanted to do something to lift her spirits. We brainstormed several ideas, and one of my team members shared an idea called a Love Run. Within her nonprofit organization, individuals nominate people who are going through a tough time. From the nominations, the board selects several people to receive a Love Run. During a Love Run, five people go to the person's home, one at a time. The first person rings the doorbell and gives the person a gift and encouraging message. A few minutes later, the second person rings the doorbell and leaves another small gift and encouraging words. This continues three more times. Then, everyone goes to the door together and gives the person a big heartfelt message of love and encouragement. We decided to adapt the idea into a Joy Run that included sending a "thinking of you" ecard that we all signed. We created and sent a short Zoom recording with everyone sharing a message of encouragement. At the end of the video, everyone held up a sign with messages such as, "Wishing you strength and peace," "Sending you lots of warm hugs," and "You were given this life because you are strong enough to live it." We also sent her a package of goodies. Our hope was that our actions would lift her spirits and bring her some moments of joy amidst her sadness. She later shared that our Joy Run really buoyed her and gave her hope for a brighter future.

How can you lift others up? Be creative. Consider having a Joy Run at your early childhood program. Deliver joyful items to staff or children. Start a Joy Run Journal and fill it with joyful pictures and messages.

In one child-care center, the director gave each member of her staff a colorful bucket to place in their room. Everyone was encouraged to write uplifting notes and place them in their coworkers' buckets. Families and children were also invited to write notes and place them in the buckets. The buckets were soon overflowing. The child-care staff felt uplifted and appreciated. The director shared how much she treasured the notes she had received. Brainstorm ideas with your team on ways you can spread joy to others and lift each other up. Working together on joyful actions will brighten everyone's day.

- Plan and implement a Joy Run or other actions that will lift someone up.
- Invite your team to join you in actions that will lift someone up.

CELEBRATE

Celebrating birthdays, holidays, and the big and small moments together is a great way to engage in joyful actions with your team. Celebrating together also helps your team members develop closer relationships. As a leader, take time to celebrate each person on your team. One way I celebrate my team members is by coming up with fun, personalized birthday gifts. One year, I found out what everyone's favorite candy was and made each person a candy cake featuring their favorite treats. Another year, I created a "box of sunshine" (a box full of sunny yellow items such as sunflowers, a yellow candle, and yellow candy). These items were joyful to create and brought joy to my team. Often, being remembered on their birthday was the most joyful part of the celebration.

There are many ways that early childhood professionals can celebrate. For example, on the first day of school at one early childhood center, all the children who attended the previous school year line up along the hallway and cheer as the new children enter the building, welcoming them to their new school. At another child-care center, the director had completed her college degree, so the staff and children planned a surprise party for her. When she entered the center, all the children and teachers greeted her, clapping and shouting congratulations as she walked down the hall. She was invited to give a short speech, and then everyone celebrated her accomplishment in the community room.

You can also take the celebration into the community. A few years ago, during the pandemic, several of my team members who teach the Child Development Associate (CDA) course created a celebration van and went to visit all the teachers who had completed the course at their home. When they arrived at each location, they used a cowbell and a megaphone to invite the teacher to come out and celebrate. They played music, ate food, and took photos. They decorated the celebration van with signs that said "CDA Celebration Van and Congratulations" and gave each teacher a certificate of completion and a small gift. They took pictures and videos and compiled them into a presentation that was shared at the virtual graduation celebration. It was a joyful and meaningful experience for everyone.

One of our local child-care centers created an extra-special experience for the children who were graduating from their preschool program. The director and teachers went to each child's house and rolled out the red carpet (literally). They brought balloons and treats for the child and had the child walk down the red carpet to receive a certificate of graduation. The individualized celebrations were greatly appreciated by the children and their families.

- Plan several ways to celebrate with the individuals you lead.
- Celebrate with the individuals you lead.

Of course, don't forget to celebrate you! Many of us are so busy taking care of the needs of others that we neglect ourselves. Take a few minutes each day to check in with yourself and see how you are doing. Self-care is not selfish; it is essential. Determine and think about what types of things that help you feel cared for during the week. Is it viewing beautiful photos, reading a book in a comfy chair, or maybe enjoying a favorite food? What matters most is how it makes you feel. If the actions boost your spirits and outlook, continue to integrate them into your daily routine.

- Spend at least five minutes engaged in an act of self-care, and celebrate you!
- Encourage your team to engage in self-care and celebrate themselves.

In summary, you can engage your team in joyful actions by developing a sense of playfulness, promoting creativity, adding joyful beginnings, engaging in selfless service, lifting each other up, and celebrating together. Engaging in joyful actions is the foundation for creating a joyful workplace culture. In the next part of this chapter, we'll delve into ways to foster joyful workplace cultures.

FOSTERING A JOYFUL WORKPLACE CULTURE

Leaders spend a great deal of time in their workplace. At times, I have wondered if my workplace was actually my second home! I have worked for organizations where I did not look forward to going to work each day because the workplace was stressful and often filled with negativity. Fortunately, my current workplace is a joyful and positive place to work, but that wasn't always the case. When I first started working there, I frequently observed confrontations among my colleagues. One of the staff members I was assigned to supervise had a negative outlook. It often felt safer to hide in my office rather than to venture out into the workspace. I struggled to defuse confrontational situations and establish a more positive and productive culture. It didn't always work out as well as I hoped; however, over time, things began to shift. There were several changes in leadership and staff, and I began to build my own team. New team members entered into a culture with expectations and beliefs that focused on positivity and joy, which guided the behavior of my team. Gradually, we created joyful habits.

Jon Gordon (2017), author of *The Power of Positive Leadership*, writes this about workplace culture: "Culture is the reason why great organizations have sustained success. Culture drives expectations and beliefs. Expectations and beliefs drive behavior. Behavior drives habits. Habits create the future." Culture is the set of rules (written or unwritten), behaviors, and characteristics of a group. The behaviors are often learned by observing others. Many of the rules and behaviors become so embedded into the culture that individuals within the group are unable to describe them. There are usually specific ways of doing things and certain behaviors that are accepted by the group as the norm. For example, in some work cultures, collaboration is valued, and most work projects are completed by a team. In other organizations, working independently is valued, and most projects are completed by individuals working alone.

Think about your workplace culture. What are the primary expectations and beliefs? What behaviors are influenced by your primary expectations and beliefs? What habits are part of your group's dynamics? If you want to create a joyful workplace culture, it is important to embrace expectations and beliefs that promote that kind of workplace.

According to Nate Dvorak and Natasha Jamal (2020), workplace culture describes how organizations do things and how individuals within organizations interact and accomplish work each day. They also identify four universal needs of healthy workplace cultures: hope, trust, compassion, and stability. Individuals within an organization need to have hope of a better future. They need to trust that words will become actions. They need to have compassion for how others feel and think and have a sense of stability.

I will add that a healthy workplace needs to include joy with team members engaging in joyful actions. As you strive to establish a joyful workplace culture, keep in mind that it is essential for people within the organization to be engaged in the practices and behaviors that reflect the culture or values you are trying to establish. In the remainder of this chapter, we'll discuss how you can do this, beginning by looking at your and your team's values.

DETERMINING YOUR VALUES

Values are the qualities or principles that are most important in our lives. Individuals within an organization tend to focus on what is valued within the company. If competition is valued, competition thrives between employees. In contrast, if collaboration is valued, collaboration is more likely to be fostered. Likewise, if joy, acts of kindness, and celebrations are valued, the team will focus on those things.

You can tell what is valued in many organizations by the type of feedback employees receive from their supervisors. If the workplace culture is built on identifying and overcoming weaknesses, supervisors will generally point out all the things that a person is doing wrong. If the workplace culture values employees' strengths, supervisors will focus on what an employee is doing right and strive to build on their strengths and promote growth and development. Your workplace culture should reflect the things that the group members value the most.

To help you determine what you value the most, try the following exercise:

- Write down what you believe are your top three values at work.
- If you had to give up one of your three values, which one would you choose to give up? It may be difficult to choose, but you need to select one value to give up.
- Now look at your two remaining values and determine which one you would give up next.
- The value that remains is your top value, followed by your second and third choices.

This exercise helps you discover the order of importance of your top three values. Being forced to choose three values and then give up two of them challenges us to be honest with ourselves about what we value the most. This exercise can help leaders examine whether they are making decisions and showing up based on what is most important or valued.
If you are having difficulty identifying your values, consider completing a personal value assessment. (I have used the Personal Values Assessment from the Barrett Values Centre.)

ALIGNING VALUES WITH ACTIONS

Once you have identified your values, consider how your actions align with them. If they are not aligned, make a concerted effort to align your actions with your values. Start by taking small and simple actions, and then move to larger and more complex actions. Share your plan with trusted colleagues, and ask them to help you keep moving forward. Over time, your actions will more closely align with your values.

Just as it will take time and effort to change your actions, it may be difficult for some team members to align their actions with your workplace culture. Individuals may be new to the organization and need more time to learn about and become comfortable with your workplace culture. Other times, the difficulty may be related to team members' personal discontent. Either way, dig deeper and support individual team members in becoming an integral part of your workplace culture.

Several years ago, I had a team member who was positive in group settings and then engaged in lots of negative talk in private conversations with other team members. As a leader, I could sense an undercurrent of negativity, but I had a hard time pinpointing the source. After having individual conversations with different team members, I learned more about what was going on. I invited the team member who was engaged in the negative talk to meet with me. We talked about her work and how things were going. She expressed several concerns and had some negative things to say about my leadership. I was surprised and a little taken aback. I listened and asked her what she needed from me. What she wanted was more of my time and attention! We discussed the core values of our workplace culture, which included using positive communication and being strengths-based and respectful. We talked about whether these values aligned with her own—she said they did—and how she could exemplify these values in her words and actions. Moreover, we set up a regular meeting schedule to talk about her work and how it aligned with our values. I became more intentional in my interactions with her. Over time, the negativity began to decrease, and she began to reflect our core values in her actions.

If you are having difficulties with anyone you lead, take time to dig deeper and find out what they need. Your situation may be more complex than giving a negative person more of your time and attention; however, when someone knows that you care about them, is willing to listen, and is open to working together to resolve the issue, you will have taken a positive first step. All your team members will benefit from determining how they can align their actions with your team's values. Consider discussing the following questions with your team:

* What do you value most about our organization's workplace culture? (Share your team values.)
* Which actions most align with our team's values?
* What types of actions do not align with our team's values?
* How can we be more intentional to ensure our actions match our team's values?
* What types of future projects would you be interested in pursuing that match our team's values?

Remember, the workplace culture is a social construct. A strong workplace is established when most team members embrace and engage in behaviors that exemplify your organization's values. Leaders can set the tone for the organization by embodying the organization's values, communicating consistent messages, and frequently reminding their team about their shared purpose and how they can work together to achieve it. Some leaders may be personable and take time to get to know their staff as both employees and individuals. Other leaders may be standoffish and have limited interactions with the individuals who work for them. The amount of positive engagement between leadership and staff can greatly influence the workplace. If leaders are critical and overly demanding, staff will prefer limited engagement with them. In contrast, if leaders are positive and encouraging, staff will look forward to higher levels of engagement with them and morale will be higher.

There is also value in bottom-up influence. If you are in a position where the leadership doesn't seem to value joy, you can instill joy within your sphere of influence. If you are a teacher, you can fill your classroom with lots of joyful moments. Your one-on-one interactions can be joyful, and you can share your positivity with others.

> Tasha's preschool room seemed brighter the moment she walked through the door. She enthusiastically greeted each child and told them how glad she was to see them. She remembered and commented on little details about each child, such as the name of their pet or favorite food. She loved playing with the children and fostering their curiosity and wonder about the world. She often brought interesting items to class, such as a Djembe drum that originated from West Africa. She told the children that the name of the Djembe drum comes from a saying that when translated means "everyone gathers together in peace." She asked the children how they could gather in peace in their classroom. The children said they could be kind and take turns. Tasha invited the children to take turns playing the Djembe drum and other interesting instruments. The children really enjoyed playing, and laughter and joy mixed with the music in Tasha's classroom. She created a joyful culture.

ESSENTIAL COMPONENTS OF A JOYFUL WORKPLACE CULTURE

These are some things that I believe are essential for a joyful workplace culture.

- **Respectful relationships:** Everyone needs to feel respected and to be respected.
- **Connections:** Team members should feel they belong and are supported by other team members.
- **Opportunities:** Team members should have opportunities to be creative and innovative.
- **Positivity:** The atmosphere should be positive, energizing, and productive.
- **Meaningful work:** Work should be meaningful and designed to make a positive difference in the lives of others.
- **Balance:** Team members should be encouraged to obtain a healthy work-life balance.

ENGAGING TEAM MEMBERS

Establishing a joyful workplace culture that reflects the team's values requires the engagement of all team members. Ongoing discussions on the topic during team meetings ensures that all members are heard. Members of my team shared that they thought a joyful workplace culture would include an environment that was free of prejudging and that contributions would be valued. My team believed that team members would engage in positive communication and cheerful greetings. They felt it would be important for individuals to be noticed and be present during interactions. They wanted to work for an organization that was respectful and authentic. Team members would honor the strengths of each person, and everyone would value equity and equality.

Think about the components that would be part of your joyful workplace culture. It may be helpful for your team to engage in reflection and discuss the following questions:

* What are the main components of a joyful workplace culture?
* What behaviors would promote joyful interactions?
* How would we build joyful connections?
* What joyful actions would we engage in with our team and others?
* How would we welcome new team members?

(Later in this chapter, I will share ideas on how you could welcome new team members.)

Determine the essential components of a joyful workplace culture with your team.

Ask your team to engage in actions that promote a joyful workplace culture.

Remember, behaviors and habits affect the culture. Within a joyful workplace culture, being respectful, supportive, and authentic lead to a sense of belonging and acceptance. As team members learn more about what others find joyful, they can talk about joyful things and engage in actions that put a smile on someone's face. As they engage in meaningful work, they will feel joyful because they will be making a positive difference in the lives of others.

JOYFUL ONBOARDING AND WELCOMING NEW TEAM MEMBERS

Fostering a joyful workplace culture begins the very first day that an individual joins your team.

How do you and your team currently welcome and onboard new personnel? The first day on a job can really set the tone for what is to follow. New hires learn a lot about what an organization values within the first few weeks of employment. New hires always face a learning curve and adjustment period, but you can ease the transition by being intentional in your onboarding process. First, set a specific time for the new person to arrive, and designate one or more individuals to meet with them and help them feel welcome. We have also implemented a number of different strategies to help the new team members feel welcome. Here are some ideas to consider:

- **Welcome basket:** Before the first day, ask the new team member to complete a Getting to Know You form. Our team uses the joyful welcome form (See appendix E.), which invites a new team member to share information on foods they find joyful, favorite colors, and hobbies or activities they enjoy. Once the form is completed, our team creates a welcome basket that includes several of the items (usually food items) that the person listed on the form. The basket is placed in the new person's workspace to welcome them to our team. This is a personal touch that lets the individual know that they belong and that we are noticing them as an individual and part of the team.
- **Greeting card:** Invite each of your team members to sign and write a short message on a card welcoming the person to the team. Place the card in the welcome basket.
- **Welcoming workspace:** Decorate the new hire's workspace or classroom in their favorite colors. Include a welcome sign and colorful streamers.
- **Joyful meeting:** On the first day or shortly thereafter, have a joyful meeting with all your team. At the meeting, everyone can share things that they find joyful. Share your teams' vision, values, and expectations. Give the new team member an opportunity to ask questions and share what they hope to accomplish in their new position.
- **Welcome document:** We created a document that includes photos of team members and a short description of each person's job title and what they find joyful. New team members have shared that it was helpful to have a document that included the mission, values, and photos of everyone on the team.
- **Welcome email:** Send an email to everyone in your organization featuring a photo of the new hire, their main job responsibilities, and a summary of things they find joyful. Invite everyone to help make the new person feel welcome.
- **Meet-and-greets:** Organize a time for the new team member to have meet-and-greets with small groups of people, such as during lunch. Invite the groups to focus their conversations on something joyful such as hobbies, memories, or adventures. The hope is that these smaller group meetings will build stronger relationships and help the team members build connections with one another.

* **Welcome buddy:** Invite one of your team members to be a welcome buddy for the new team member. This person becomes the new colleague's go-to person for questions and concerns. The welcome buddy could set up a weekly get-together and do daily check-ins with the new person for the first couple of weeks. One of the main roles of the welcome buddy is to help the new person navigate the workplace culture and support them as they acclimate to their position. Having a go-to person can really help new team members feel comfortable and gain an understanding of the unwritten norms that are often associated with workplace cultures.
* **One-month milestone:** Recognize the new team member's one-month milestone. The recognition could include a fun certificate or special treat. As a joyful leader, meet one on one with the new person to find out what is going well and if they have any concerns that require additional assistance. Ask them to share how things are going with their welcome buddy and if they need any additional professional learning opportunities to help them with their position. Share your appreciation for how they are becoming a valuable member of your team. Be authentic and sincere.
* **Secret friends:** Invite several of your team members to be the new team member's secret friend for the first couple of months. The role of a secret friend is to leave encouraging messages in the person's workspace, to pay attention if the person needs assistance, and to go the extra mile in engaging in joyful interactions with them. The secret friends are asked to serve the person in whatever way they think will bring them joy. The hope is that after a couple of months, the team members will continue to want to bring joy to each other. This is a great way to have several people looking out for the new person if there is not a more formalized role such as being a buddy or mentor.
* **Random acts of joy:** Invite all your team to engage in at least one random act of joy for the new team member. This way, everyone is involved in continuing to help the new person feel welcome. If you have a large team, you could divide it up and assign several people to each week of the month so that the joyfulness is ongoing throughout the month.

These ideas are designed to get you thinking about different ways that you could joyfully welcome a new person onto your team. Start by implementing just one of the ideas. Once it is established, consider adding additional ideas. I asked for volunteers from my team to help organize and implement the ideas because joyful leaders know how to delegate.

Because we hire only a few new people each year, we expanded our focus and adapted some of the ideas to build stronger relationships within our team. We designated one month as Random Acts of Joy month. During the month, everyone was invited to try to do one random act of joy for each person on our team. Creating a joyful workplace culture is an ongoing process. Periodically, invite team members to think of additional ways to enhance your workplace culture. Another way we have enhanced our workplace culture has been by creating joyful environments.

DESIGNING JOYFUL ENVIRONMENTS

Sometimes, just adding some colorful décor to your workplace can make the environment more joyful. At our office, the workplace break area was functional but lacked joy. We started simply. We began by posting joyful quotes that we changed every few weeks and decorating the refrigerator with vinyl clings.

Next, our team created and set up joyful displays, such as simple decorated jars of silk flowers on colorful place mats, in several strategic locations within our workplace. Team members were encouraged to personalize their cubicles with family photos, message blocks, and interesting décor, which enabled each person to share their interests and personality through their environment.

Some additional ways to enhance your workplace environment could include making a joyful memories' bulletin board featuring pictures of the team engaged in fun activities or creating a photo collage on a specific topic such as My Life with Pets. Be creative. What could you do to make your environment more joyful? What colors are found in the workplace? Is everything neutral, or are there splashes of color and interesting designs? Is the environment stark or personalized? What are some simple ways that your workplace environment could be more joyful?

- Add one item to your workplace environment to make it more joyful.
- Invite your team to add items to the workplace environment that they find joyful.

This chapter has been full of ideas on how you and your team can take joyful actions together. You are encouraged to use these ideas as a springboard for coming up with your own ideas for how your team can engage in joyful actions and create a more joyful workplace culture.

DISCUSSION QUESTIONS

1. What are two examples of joyful actions that you have seen in your program or classroom?

____

____

____

2. How could you invite and involve your team in a joyful journey?

____

____

____

3. What are some benefits of engaging your team in playfulness?

____

____

____

4. Which joyful-beginning ideas resonated with you?

____

____

____

5. How has, or could, your team engage in selfless service?

____

____

____

6. What are some uplifting ways your team could work together?

7. What are three things your team could celebrate?

8. How could you promote creativity with your team?

9. Think about your workplace culture. What does the leadership view as important?

10. What are some ways you currently welcome new staff? Are there any additional ideas you would like to implement? If yes, what would you like to do?

REFLECTION ACTIVITY: TWO CLICKS AND ONE CLUNK

- Write down two "clicks" (two things that resonate with you) from the chapter.

____

____

____

- Write down one "clunk" (an idea that does not resonate with you or that you have questions about).

____

____

____

ACTION PLAN

Determine one or more actions you will take this month to engage in joyful actions.

- Action:

  ____

  ____

  ____

- Why is this action important?

  ____

  ____

  ____

- What are my next steps?

  ____

  ____

  ____

CHAPTER 5

Create Caring Connections

"Alone we can do so little; together we can do so much."

—*Helen Keller,* author and disability rights advocate

You rise as a leader as you create caring connections with your team. As Helen Keller writes, together we can do so much. Teams can do so such more than one person can do alone. By creating caring connections with each other, team members are able to work together effectively and productively. In this chapter, we'll discuss how to create caring connections and also look at how leaders become caring communicators.

FOUR WAYS TO CREATE CARING CONNECTIONS

Fred Rogers (1995) says, "Our job in life is to help people realize how rare and valuable each one of us really is." As leaders, we should strive to create caring connections with each member of our team. Individuals who engage in positive interactions are more likely to display trust, empathy, and compassion (Houston, 2019; Rosales, 2016). We have a human need to feel connected. Creating caring connections with others is essential to our well-being both socially and emotionally.

Ways to create caring connections include:

* building trust and a sense of belonging within your team,
* being authentic and vulnerable,
* demonstrating respect and sensitivity to others, and
* seeking diverse viewpoints and overcoming challenges together.

"By behaving in ways that build trust with one, you build trust with many."

—Stephen M. R. Covey, (2018)

BUILDING TRUST AND A SENSE OF BELONGING

An essential practice of joyful leadership is to build trust and a sense of belonging with the individuals that you lead. Belonging is more than just including others. Leaders need to be intentional in creating a shared feeling of community with their team, which is developed when they value team members' contributions. Team members need to know that you care about them and that you trust them to follow through and accomplish what needs to be done.

Trust begins to form when you let others into your personal space and engage in conversations that are authentic and open. You can build this trust by being an active listener; trusting them first; being consistent, honest, and transparent; and accepting and valuing the strengths of all your team members.

Building trust does involve risk. It can be upsetting when someone breaks your trust, yet it's important to have an honest conversation about what happened because that person may not have done so intentionally. If the person is sincere and apologetic, give them opportunities to rebuild your trust. It is best not to hold someone's past failure over their head indefinitely.

Some team members may have a hard time fully trusting their leaders because of their own fears. For example, one of my team members was fearful about sharing a professional struggle she was experiencing. She was working on passing a certification test and felt she should be able to meet the challenge without help. The test allows for three attempts to pass, and support is available from the certifying organization, if requested. Unfortunately, my team member did not reach out for assistance and failed all three attempts, which meant that she would need to retake a training course and go through the recertification process again. Although this was not a positive outcome for her, it opened new opportunities for her to build higher levels of trust so that she would be more comfortable seeking support in the future. She later acknowledged that she wished she had been more open about her struggle because she believed it would have resulted in a different outcome. She committed to being more open with her struggles in the future. This experience reminded me that we cannot assume that all our team members feel emotionally safe. It takes time and intentional action to build and maintain trust. It is essential to have regular check-ins with the individuals you lead and to engage in ongoing actions that build trust and a sense of belonging.

One way our team has built trust and a sense of belonging is through one- to two-day semi-annual retreats. Before the retreats, the team gives input on the types of experiences they would like to have during our time together. At one of our December retreats, we completed a book-cleaning service project, visited a beautiful flower display (which gave us opportunities for joyspotting), ate a delicious lunch, and then shared our one word for the next year. This shared experience built meaningful connections among team members.

Leaders can build on this trust and create a stronger sense of belonging by keeping confidences and allowing team members to be vulnerable. For example, provide team members with opportunities to share both positive and negative feelings. Sometimes, team members just need to vent about the frustrations they are experiencing; however, try to limit the time spent on negativity and spend more time focused on thinking of solutions. Make sure team members have all the facts or the correct information. They will feel more secure when their leaders are transparent and keep them informed about what is happening within the organization. Some questions that can start a productive conversation with team members include the following:

- What do you like most about your position?
- What motivates you to do your best work?
- In what areas do you feel your performance is strongest?
- What will you focus on this month and/or year to help you grow and develop?
- What can I do to support your performance and development?
- What, if any, concerns would you like to discuss? What is the best way to address your concerns?

These types of questions focus primarily on the positive aspects of the individual's position. They also give team members an opportunity to share their concerns. During one of my conversations with a team member, she shared a concern about not receiving a raise in several years, and she was finding it harder to meet increasing cost-of-living expenses. I validated her concern, told her I appreciated her sharing it with me, and said I would explore some options. I knew there would be hurdles within the organization, but I reached out to the human resources department and approached our funders about increasing salaries in the future. I was pleasantly surprised that the funders felt I was making a responsible request. Although it took about a year to come to fruition, team members received salary increases. I was grateful that my team member shared her concern and trusted that I would act on her concern.

Building a culture of trust within your organization has several benefits. According to research conducted by Paul Zak (2017), founding director of the Center for Neuroeconomics Studies at Claremont Graduate University, "People at high-trust companies reported 74 percent less stress, 106 percent more energy at work, 50 percent higher productivity, 13 percent fewer sick days, 76 percent more engagement, 29 percent more satisfaction with their lives, and 40 percent less burnout" when compared with people at low-trust companies. Trust can make a big difference in the productivity, quality of work, and engagement of your team.

Consider these additional ways to build trust:

- Show trust by giving your team members opportunities to take on enhanced responsibilities without your interference. Remember, the outcome is more important than how they get to the end result.
- Show appreciation in the ways that the individual feels appreciated. For example, send a thank-you card or treat them to lunch.
- Nominate team members for awards, and publicly or privately recognize their accomplishments when they shine. After one of our team members received a collaboration award, she said, "I was so surprised and thankful to be noticed for my hard work."
- Let others know that you are proud of what your team members have accomplished.
- Show and tell your team members, "You belong here. I am glad you are part of our team." This action should be ongoing. Create a culture that continuously builds trust and belonging.

Select one way to build trust and a sense of belonging with your team, and then do it.

Invite your team to engage in actions that will build trust and a sense of belonging in your team.

"Staying vulnerable is a risk we have to take if we want to experience connection."

—**Brené Brown** (2010)

BEING AUTHENTIC AND VULNERABLE

Authenticity and vulnerability can help leaders create joyful and caring connections. Leaders' willingness to be authentic and vulnerable helps team members feel more comfortable sharing their feelings, insights, and ideas. Have courage to go outside your comfort zone and connect with others. In the past, I have struggled with sharing personal aspects of my life with others. As I became a more joyful leader, I found that I wanted to share more about myself and what brought me joy. In turn, as I shared stories about my family and our adventures, I noticed that others were doing the same. I learned much more about the people on my team as they began sharing stories about their travels, families, pets, and interests. With time, I became more comfortable sharing both my joys and struggles. I became authentic and vulnerable as I shared more about myself, my thoughts, and my feelings. My training sessions and interactions with others has become more relatable and meaningful.

Your team can create caring connections by going through good and bad times together. It is usually better to laugh than cry, yet I have made some strong connections with others when tears were shed. When my mother passed away, the love and support I received from others helped me grieve my loss and gain the strength to move forward. I was authentic and vulnerable and acknowledged my grief. This loss also helped me gain greater empathy for others who had experienced similar losses. Giving your team love, empathy, and compassion during the hard times deepens relationships and strengthens your team—and makes the good times even sweeter.

Being authentic and vulnerable does not mean you need to share everything with your team. Be selective and determine which stories would be appropriate for the listeners. Share a fun story from your childhood or an experience you had with a friend. Stories of our lives help others learn more about who we really are and what is important to us. Teachers can build relationships with families by sharing aspects of their lives and talking about things that they find joyful. One teacher likes to share stories about her dog Baxter. The children love to see pictures and hear stories about the adventures she takes with him. The children also like to share stories about their pets. Stories build connections. Encourage the individuals you lead to share their stories. Be curious and open to learning more about them. Be present and seek to find commonalities. Be authentic and vulnerable and discuss both difficulties and blessings.

One of the challenges our team has faced within its work was trying to determine the best ways to address the low morale within the early childhood field. Even though child-care providers are essential workers, many issues and concerns within the field remain unresolved. High turnover rates, stressful work conditions, burnout, and low wages are real and ongoing. My team members train and coach early childhood teachers and have seen firsthand the difficulties directors, teachers, and families are facing. My team has noticed that many teachers have a much more negative view of themselves than they have had in the past, and it has been harder to help them find joy when they are immersed in stressful situations.

As a team, we discussed different strategies we could try. One that our team implemented was offering virtual care circles for teachers. Care circles are specific times when teachers can meet with a coach in a small-group setting. They are designed for facilitating conversations with teachers and providing them with care and support. My team said it is joyful to have these authentic conversations. They feel they have been able to give the teachers hope, as the teachers feel supported as they come together and share their ideas and concerns within a safe space. Even if the challenges have not gone away, the teachers feel care and kindness from our team members.

It can also be helpful to find humor in the unexpected and to share what happened with your team. Even embarrassing moments can seem less humiliating when you find the humor in them. A few years ago, I invited my team to meet for lunch at a restaurant. I arrived at the restaurant early so that I could set up the environment with little thank-you items for each person. Noon arrived and no one came. I wondered if I had the wrong day. No, I had the right day. Then I realized I had the wrong time! The lunch was at 1:00 p.m., not noon! I debated about what to do. Should I just sit at the table for an hour or leave? I decided to leave and do some errands. So I gathered everything, went out the door, and then came back an hour later and set up everything again. I shared this story with my team members, and we all had a laugh about it. This story reflected my humanness. I was authentic and vulnerable. None of my team would have known what happened if I hadn't shared my story. This opened the opportunity for others to share stories about the unexpected and silly things they had done in the past, which deepened our relationships.

Joyful leaders can ask others to share stories about things that matter most to them. It is important that the topic for the story be intentionally phrased to focus on the positive aspects of the subject. For example, you could ask a teacher to tell a story about the best learning moment she has had with the children in her class. After she has shared the story, ask her to dig a little deeper by answering some follow-up questions, such as, "How did you feel during this learning moment?" "How did the children feel?" "Why does this experience stand out?" "What were the key factors and conditions that existed during this learning moment?" These types of questions can deepen the exchange and enrich the conversation. Notice that you are asking the person to share their feelings about the experience and why it was important to them.

Find opportunities to be authentic and vulnerable with your team. Share a story about yourself with your team.

Invite the individuals that you lead to share their stories with each other.

DEMONSTRATING RESPECT AND SENSITIVITY TO OTHERS

Leaders create caring connections when they demonstrate respect and sensitivity to others. To me, being respectful is treating others with dignity. I feel respected when other people consider my thoughts and feelings. They may not agree with me, but they can respectfully listen to what I have to say. It is best when respect is mutual; the Dalai Lama has said, "Mutual respect is the foundation of genuine harmony" (Tenzin, 2001). When team members are respectful and sensitive to the needs of others, harmony is created within your team. Respect and sensitivity are also exhibited as your team members work with others, as seen in the following example of an early childhood coach.

> Shanice had a teacher in her CDA credential program who was ready to give up and quit. Alexis was having difficulty writing her competency statements, which is a requirement for the credential. When Shanice called her, Alexis was distressed. Shanice asked her to just share her thoughts about one of the competency statements. Alexis talked, and Shanice listened and wrote down what she said. After the call, Shanice typed up what Alexis had told her and sent the notes to her. Alexis cried as she read her statements; the notes expressed what she had been unable to write. She had it in her, and she was competent; however, the task needed to be modified so that she could find success in her work.

Leaders can have a powerful effect on someone when they pivot what they do for each person, based on that person's needs.

Another way to demonstrate respect and sensitivity to others is to admit that you are wrong. We all make mistakes, and it's especially important for leaders to own up to mistakes they make that affect others. I have overreacted at times and needed to apologize. Likewise, I have made inaccurate assumptions and later had to retract my words because I jumped to conclusions without all the facts. Can you relate? Leaders sometimes make mistakes because they don't always perceive the situation correctly. Shawn Achor (2010), author of *The Happiness Advantage*, says, "Our interpretation of reality changes our experience of that reality." When I am stressed, I have a more negative outlook; whereas, when things are going well, my outlook is more positive. Our perceptions often become our reality. For example, imagine a large dog is running toward you. Do you perceive a big beast coming to attack and therefore cower in fear? Or do you perceive a bundle of furry fun and leap forward to play with the dog? Our perceptions and reactions are often based on our experiences, and these perceptions can influence how we approach a situation. Because of their knowledge and experiences, leaders sometimes face situations that they perceive differently than others do. It is important to recognize that your team members may perceive situations through a different lens than your own; be sure to acknowledge those differences.

The most effective leaders acknowledge and admit their mistakes and move forward. The faster you right a wrong, the faster it is forgotten. When people have time to stew and brew, those negative feelings grow and fester. But when wrongs are taken care of quickly, individuals usually can forgive and forget.

A few years ago, my team received a complaint from another team that the conference room had been left in a mess, and they believed our team had used the room last. Instead of arguing or denying the allegation, we worked quickly to resolve the issue. It didn't matter whether we were in the right or wrong. Action was needed, and we cleaned up the mess. When faced with an issue, I have found that it is best to quickly develop a solution, fix it, and move on. Complainants are quickly pacified when the focus is shifted from the complaint to resolving the issue. Leaders are better off spending more time on resolving issues and less time on being right.

- Determine one way you can be respectful and sensitive to others.
- Admit your mistakes and work with your team to resolve issues quickly.

SEEKING DIVERSE VIEWPOINTS AND OVERCOMING CHALLENGES TOGETHER

Seeking diverse viewpoints is another way to create caring connections. In 2020, when the issue of racial inequity was at the forefront of national discourse, I invited one of our team members to lead a discussion on the topic from her perspective. She selected some articles and videos that our team could read and view prior to our meeting. She used resources from the National Association for the Education of Young Children (NAEYC) website and books such as *Don't Look Away: Embracing Anti-Bias Classrooms* (Iruka, Curenton, Durden, and Escayg, 2020). She began her remarks by stating that some of the things she was going to share might be uncomfortable, but she hoped we could have a respectful discussion focused on each person's thoughts and feelings. Our team had an emotional conversation. Feelings were shared, tears were shed, and minds were enlightened.

"A diverse mix of voices leads to better discussions, decisions, and outcomes for everyone."

—**Sundar Pichai,** CEO of Alphabet, Inc., and Google

The initial conversation on social justice led to an increased awareness of the issue by team members. We determined that we would continue to revisit the topic monthly and learn and grow together through participating in a training program focused on diversity and inclusion. One interesting discussion during our training was related to grouping and how we quickly categorize people into our "in group" (people who are like ourselves) and "out group" (people who are different from us). We talked about how, when you first meet a person, they are in your "out group" until you identify similarities and make connections. As you begin to see how the person is like yourself, they become part of your "in group." Finding similarities with others is a key to having meaningful conversations. I remember meeting an individual from another culture who, upon first appearances, seemed very different from me. We began a conversation and quickly learned that we were both grandparents, and we loved working on issues related to early childhood. This person quickly moved from my "out group" to my "in group" as we had a meaningful conversation and learned about our similarities. We felt connected and had a greater appreciation for the differences that made each of us unique. By seeking diverse viewpoints, I gained new perspectives and began to think about diversity and inclusion in a new light. We can give only what we have been given, and it important to be open to learning new knowledge and skills to strengthen our leadership abilities.

As a leader, it is sometimes important to ask yourself, "What do I need to *un*learn?" I had to unlearn a habit of primarily focusing on what was going wrong and learn how to focus more on what was working. I had to unlearn getting stuck in a negative mindset and learn how to be more positive and joyful. Within the early childhood field, I have observed some teachers and directors who needed to unlearn some of the ways they spoke and interacted with young children, families, and staff. I remember coaching a new lead preschool teacher who was using lots of negative language with the children in her class. During a thirty-minute observation, I observed her saying the word *don't* more than a dozen times. As we talked about the observation, I could tell she was frustrated, and she told me that she was thinking about quitting her job. I asked her if she was interested in strengthening her classroom-management skills and learning new ways to interact with the children. She said she was, and we began working to strengthen her skills. She had to unlearn some of her habits in how she spoke to children and guided their behavior. It took time, but she was diligent in her efforts. She became a more joyful teacher, and the children in her class were happier as well.

"It is not our differences that divide us. It is our inability to recognize, accept, and celebrate those differences."

—**Audre Lorde** (2007)

- Identify something that you need to unlearn, and determine what you need to learn instead.
- Ask your team members to identify something they need to unlearn and what they need to learn instead.

As a leader, you may face a range of challenges within your team, such as personality clashes among team members, disengaged team members, and negativity. It is best if these challenges are addressed head on. Name the elephant in the room and work together to determine how to best approach the issue. Look for underlying causes, and create a positive atmosphere focused on solutions. Sometimes, it is best to find out more information about a situation before you bring the challenge to your team (for example, an isolated incident of uncharacteristic behavior that you can address with the individual).

One strategy for addressing challenges within a team is through group problem solving. The leader brings the team together, poses the problem, and then encourages everyone to offer ideas on how to resolve the challenge. This can be empowering to team members as they brainstorm and work together to determine a solution. Let's see how this worked in action at one early childhood organization.

> One of Fatima's team members, Ah Lam, was going to be out for an extended period following surgery. Instead of trying to figure it out herself, Fatima set aside some time to bring the team together to discuss the challenge and determine what they should do. She encouraged everyone to think creatively. They outlined the essential tasks and those that could wait until Ah Lam returned to work. Different colleagues volunteered to take on tasks. There was some give-and-take to distribute the tasks as fairly as possible. Fatima also discussed what obligations the team members could set aside, so they had time for the new tasks. Although there were many details to consider, Fatima and her team met the challenge because everyone was willing to do their part (even if that meant doing something extra).

As some tasks were unique to Ah Lam, Fatima set up time for training sessions before Ah Lam went out on leave. Did everything go smoothly while Ah Lam was gone? No, but Fatima and her team addressed the issues the best they could during her absence. Fatima was confident that things went better because they engaged in group problem solving before Ah Lam left.

If you are facing challenges in your team, try the following steps:

- Set aside time to discuss challenges and resolutions.
- Create an atmosphere that promotes creative thought. Be open to all kinds of solutions, even if they seem improbable. Divergent thinking can often lead to the best solutions.
- Take time to dig deeper. Examine underlying causes and effects.
- Determine the key issue and select a potential solution.
- Delegate tasks designed to resolve the issue.
- Set a time to regroup and report on progress. Continue to meet as needed, until the issue is resolved.

Determine a challenge that your team could overcome together.

Guide your team in the process as they overcome a challenge together.

For teams to overcome challenges, learn, and grow, they must spend some time outside their comfort zones. Becoming uncomfortable is an important step in broadening perspective and becoming more open to diverse viewpoints. If everyone thinks the same way, programming and progress will be limited to like-minded thoughts and ideas.

Diverse viewpoints convey unique perspectives that early childhood leaders and teachers need to consider. Within a child-care setting, the administrative team may not truly understand the viewpoints and concerns of the teachers or the families in their programs unless they seek input from these individuals. It can be helpful to spend a day walking in someone else's shoes to truly understand what they are experiencing. A few years ago, I watched an episode of the TV show *Undercover Boss*, which involves having the leader of a company wear a disguise and spend time as an employee in that company. The leader attempts to do the job of one of the staff he or she directs. In one of the episodes, the chief executive of a food company that sells cinnamon rolls spent some time working on the front line in a store, and she failed miserably. When she was interviewed after the experience, she shared that the job was much harder than she had imagined, and she had gained greater respect for her employees. She was surprised by the number of responsibilities her employees needed to manage. She even said she would probably have fired herself, as she had made some significant blunders. Moreover, she appreciated how patient her young "boss" had been with her. She gained some new insights, and her perspective about training, protocols, and expectations shifted.

Likewise, as early childhood leaders, we need to be open to the perspectives of teachers, families, and children. We may need a refresher course on the challenges early childhood educators face each day. As you seek to understand the perspectives of others, you will gain an authentic appreciation for differing points of view. Be open to seeing situations from the viewpoint of others and reflect on how open you are to views that differ from your own. Consider these strategies:

- Be curious and ask thoughtful questions.
- Learn more about the stories of each person on your team. Ask team members to share their stories with each other.
- Actively solicit input from individuals with diverse perspectives from both within and outside of your team. Listen carefully to their thoughts and viewpoints.
- Ask individuals with diverse viewpoints to walk you through their thought process, which can lead to greater understanding and acceptance.
- Spend some time walking in someone else's shoes to truly understand what they are experiencing.

Seek diverse viewpoints from your team and others on a relevant issue.

Give your team opportunities to explore and discuss diverse viewpoints.

In this section, we explored ways to create caring connections. Leaders do this as they build trust and a sense of belonging within their team through authenticity, vulnerability, seeking diverse viewpoints, demonstrating respect and sensitivity to others, and admitting when they are wrong. In the next section, we'll explore another aspect of creating caring connections: becoming a caring communicator.

CARING COMMUNICATION

To be a caring communicator requires you to thoughtfully consider the impact of your words and actions on others. It includes caring about what you say and how you say it. Caring communicators exchange ideas in a thoughtful and considerate manner. They listen intently to what is being said and pay attention to nonverbal communication. Caring communicators seek to gain a greater understanding of the meaning behind the words and actions of others. Stephen R. Covey (2004), author of *The 7 Habits of Highly Effective People*, says, "Seek first to understand, then to be understood." Leaders make strong connections within their team when they strive to communicate with care. They engage in caring communication as they exude warmth and positive energy, choose their words carefully, use strengths-based language, and ask intentional questions.

EXUDE WARMTH AND POSITIVE ENERGY

Communication is more than just the words that are spoken. It is also the emotions that are connected to the words. One of my team members has the gift of creating a positive connection with everyone she meets. She exudes warmth and positive energy. People are drawn to her, and they look forward to being in her presence. She has the ability to lift your spirits as she happily greets you and tells you she is so glad to see you. She radiates joy with her upbeat personality. People want to be near positive and joyful individuals. Positive energy is contagious. It is uplifting and infuses joyfulness into the atmosphere.

"If you have good thoughts, they will shine out of your face like sunbeams, and you will always look lovely."

—**Roald Dahl** (1980)

Early childhood leaders and teachers can set the example of how to be caring communicators through modeling simple actions, such as smiling at team members, families, and children and by giving each person a sincere greeting. Leaders take time to talk with team members about upcoming plans and projects and seek to ensure that the meaning of their words and actions is understood. They give feedback in a kind and thoughtful manner and listen to the feedback they receive from others. Joyful leaders exude warmth and positive energy.

Here are a few ways you can exude this energy as you interact with others.

- Smile and joyfully make eye contact, if culturally appropriate to do so.
- Use the person's name in conversation to help them feel connected.
- Ensure you have open body language. Avoid crossing your arms or legs when conversing, as that can be perceived as a gesture to protect or distance yourself from someone else.
- Be present and actively listen, and tune in for possible connections. What is important to the person you are listening to? What interests them? Be genuine in learning more about them.

Make a conscious effort to exude warmth and positive energy as you engage in caring communication with your team.

Invite your team to engage in caring communication with each other.

CHOOSE YOUR WORDS

Caring communicators know their words can influence how others feel and what they do. Words are powerful, whether they are spoken or written. Instead of asking, "How was your day?" and hearing the rote reply, "Fine," ask an open-ended questions such as, "What happened today that put a smile on your face?" One of my team members asks her children this question every day when they come home from school, and it has made a big difference in how they respond. Her children to pay more attention to the things that make them smile. In fact, thinking about how to answer that question shifts a person's thought process into a positive mindset. One way that I shifted to a more joyful mindset is by closing my emails with statements such as, "Have a joyful day," and "May your week be full of joy." I always smile as I type the words. I am still amazed at how including the words *joy* and *joyful* in my speech and written word continues to remind me to be joyful!

Using different words to describe a situation can lead to different outcomes. Think about how you feel when someone tells you that you *must* do something. Do you feel any resistance to complying with the command? I know I would. What if instead you were *invited* to do something? How would you feel? *Invite* is a powerful word. If you recall, at the beginning of this book I invited you to go on a joyful journey. Being invited gives a person the autonomy to make a choice. You feel respected. I have had greater participation within my team when I intentionally invite everyone to participate and let them know it is okay to pass. I also ask, "Who is willing to share an idea?" instead of "Who would like to share an idea?" People are often willing to share even if they do not like sharing. The use of the word *willing* has also led to higher levels of participation. Instead of asking if anyone has any questions, I ask, "Is there anything that I can clarify?" This shifts the responsibility to you as the questioner to clarify the information, instead of focusing on the individual asking a question and making them feel that they did not understand what you said.

USE STRENGTHS-BASED LANGUAGE

Caring communication centers on what the person is doing well, and using strengths-based language ensures that your words focus on the positive instead of the negative. For example, instead of describing a situation as a problem, describe it as an opportunity to learn and overcome a challenge.

> Anya was an exuberant child in Malik's classroom. She had difficulty understanding personal boundaries and loved to hug other children, which was sometimes unwanted and problematic. Instead of focusing on the negative aspects of Anya's behavior, Malik used strengths-based language to describe the behavior: "Anya is affectionate and wants to show her peers that she likes them." Malik honored Anya's strength by helping her learn how to share her affection in different ways. He taught her to ask her peers whether they wanted a hug, a fist bump, or a big smile. This helped Anya connect with her peers in acceptable ways.

As a leader you can use strength-based questions to learn more about your team members. Try asking your team these types of questions:

- What energizes you at work?
- Describe a productive day. What made it productive?
- What is the most rewarding aspect of your job?
- What inspires you to do your best work?
- What's working well for you?
- What part of your job do you enjoy the most?

These are just a few examples of how the words you choose to use can influence your interactions with others. Strengths-based language creates caring connections and honors the unique strengths of each person.

ASK INTENTIONAL QUESTIONS

In addition to using strengths-based language, caring communicators ask intentional questions. Have you ever been asked a question and become immediately upset? Ronald Fry, professor of organization behavior at Case Western Reserve University, has said that we need to treat questions as fateful or as having the potential for unintentional consequences. In his course Leading Positive Change through Appreciative Inquiry, he further stated that there is no such thing as a neutral question. The words we use can influence the actions of others. Fry gives the example of a pharmacist assistant who decided to track the difference in responses she received based on what she said. When individuals picked up their prescriptions and she said, "Call me in a few days and tell me how you are doing," about half of the follow-up calls were positive and about half were negative. When she changed her statement by one word and said, "Call me in a few days and tell me how well you are doing," about 80 percent of the calls were positive. Could one word really be so powerful that it would influence how people respond? Do your own experiment and see if you notice any differences based on how you ask questions. What are the results when you ask a question focused on the positive versus a neutral or negative question?

Intentional questions can help team members explore and discover what factors are present when they are at their best. Some examples of intentional questions that early childhood leaders could ask include the following:

- How did your strengths contribute to the positive outcomes of the children in your classroom?
- What is the best thing about working for this program?
- What makes your teaching team the best it can be?
- What does your program do exceptionally well in meeting the needs of children and families?
- What ideas from our meeting were the most valuable?

As you can see from these questions, they are deliberately guiding the respondent to focus on positive aspects of their profession. Consider incorporating a few of these questions in an upcoming meeting, and then discuss the responses with your team.

- Practice writing three intentional questions that you could ask the individuals you lead. Experiment with asking the intentionally strengths-based questions and reflect on what happens.

- Invite your team to write three intentional questions and reflect on them. Encourage them to ask the intentionally strengths-based questions and reflect on what happens.

As a joyful leader, one of my expectations is to have ongoing caring connections with my team members. Author John O'Leary (2016) says, "Our expectations shape our world." If you expect to lead with care and joy, you will lead with care and joy. As a joyful leader, you can guide your team to create caring connections as you build trust, are authentic and vulnerable, demonstrate respect and sensitivity to others, seek diverse viewpoints, and engage in caring communication.

DISCUSSION QUESTIONS

1. What could you do to create stronger caring connections with members of your team?

2. How could you help the individuals you lead create stronger connections with each other?

3. How do you currently build trust and a sense of belonging within your team? What else could you do?

4. How could you be more authentic and vulnerable with your team?

5. How do you demonstrate respect and sensitivity to your team members?

6. What strategies do you use to resolve issues?

____

____

____

7. What have you learned from seeking diverse viewpoints?

____

____

____

8. Which of the following are strengths, and which are opportunities for growth?
    - Exuding warmth and positive energy
    - Choosing words carefully
    - Using strengths-based language
    - Asking intentional questions

____

____

____

9. What is one way you could strengthen your caring communication as a leader?

____

____

____

REFLECTION ACTIVITY: TWO RECALLS, TWO INSIGHTS, TWO ACTIONS

- Two recalls: Write down two main ideas or recalls from the reading.

  ____

  ____

  ____

- Two insights: Write down two insights from the reading.

  ____

  ____

  ____

- Two actions: Write down two actions you could take based on the reading.

  ____

  ____

  ____

ACTION PLAN

Determine one or more actions you will take this month to create caring connections.

* Action:

  ____

  ____

  ____

* Why is this action important?

  ____

  ____

  ____

* What are my next steps?

  ____

  ____

  ____

CHAPTER 6

Use Reflection to Build Strengths

"Self-reflection is the school of wisdom."

—*Baltasar Gracián* (1992)

You rise as a leader as you use reflection—thinking deeply about your thoughts, ideas, and opinions—to build not only your strengths as a leader and teacher but also the strengths of your team members. Reflection can have a powerful influence on what we think and what we do. Let's take a peek into one preschool classroom to see how reflection helped two teachers to build on their strengths.

> Trina, a lead teacher in a preschool classroom, and Andrea, her assistant teacher, had worked well together for several years. Then, Andrea became irritated and frustrated with the administration at their child-care center. Andrea's strong emotions began affecting her mental and physical health.

In fact, her frustration had started to spill into her interactions with the children in the classroom. This concerned Trina; she had tried talking to Andrea about her concerns, but the conversations had not gone well. Trina wasn't sure what to do. She took some time to reflect on how she could best support Andrea. She hoped she could find some ways to help alleviate her colleague's frustration and stress.

Trina brought Andrea a small gift and a thank-you card expressing her appreciation for having her as an assistant teacher. Trina also began pointing out the positive moments they were having during the day and how their actions made a difference in the children's lives. Andrea did better for a couple of days, but then she became irritable again. Trina asked Andrea if she would be willing to do some reflection. Andrea said she would. Trina asked her to take some time and reflect on what really mattered most to her as a preschool teacher and, when she was ready, to share her thoughts.

A few days later, Andrea told Trina she was ready to share. She said that what mattered the most to her was helping children become excited about learning new things. As she spoke, Andrea realized her frustration and irritation about things that were going on outside the classroom were affecting what she was doing in the classroom. She apologized to Trina and promised to stay focused on what was most important and not let her emotions affect her interactions with the children. Trina gave her a hug and thanked her again for being her assistant teacher.

After their discussion, Andrea started having a more positive attitude in the classroom. She began having more joyful interactions with the children, and she told Trina that the issues with the administration seemed less bothersome now that she was focusing on what mattered most.

Reflection helped Trina come up with ways to support Andrea, and reflection helped Andrea determine what mattered the most to her as a preschool teacher. Each found the joyful leader within herself.

Write down your reflections about a leader who had a positive influence on you and your leadership. What were the leader's strengths? What did they do that made a difference?

Invite your team to reflect on leaders who have had a positive influence on them. What were the leader's strengths? What did they do that made a difference?

Many leaders who have positively influenced me have had similar characteristics, including the following:

* **Authenticity:** As an authentic leader, they admitted when they had made a mistake. They had empathy for others.
* **Generosity:** As a generous leader, they were willing to take on any task within the organization, from mopping the floor to covering someone else's shift. They exhibited openness and adaptability. They were generous with their praise.
* **Courage:** As a courageous leader, they stood up for doing the right thing. They brought people together for a shared cause. They made tough decisions and courageously explained why they took certain actions.

- **Focusing on strengths:** As a strengths-based leader, they noticed what a person was doing well, even if that person was struggling. They saw the positive intent behind the actions of others and focused on how they could enhance and build on the strengths of others.
- **Being transformational:** As a transformational leader, they made lasting, sustainable changes within their organization and the community. They had a clear purpose and vision. Their efforts resulted in positive outcomes.
- **Joy:** As a joyful leader, they spread optimism, even during tough times. They lifted and guided the individuals they led and helped others look for and find joy.
- **Gratitude:** As a grateful leader, they were thankful for the people and things that they had in their life. They expressed gratitude for their team and recognized each person's efforts.
- **Creativity:** As a creative leader, they had the ability to think outside the box and find creative solutions to issues. They used a positive framework for finding solutions to problems. They were innovative and forward thinking.
- **Relationship builders:** As a relationship-building leader, they were connected to the individuals they led and established genuine bonds with their team. They took time to establish a relationship with each person that was built on trust and mutual respect.

The characteristics and strengths that you identified may be different from what I identified. The important thing is to reflect on how these leaders had a positive influence on you and how you are emulating these behaviors in your leadership.

FINDING TIME FOR REFLECTION

Within our busy lives, it can sometimes be hard to find quiet time. I have found that my reflection is more insightful when I can be still in a quiet and peaceful atmosphere and let my thoughts flow. You may need to be creative in finding small pockets of time when you can escape the busyness of the day, block out distractions, and reflect. When do you do your best reflection? First thing in the morning? At the end of the day? Throughout the day? What's important is taking time to reflect.

- Find some time for reflection.
- Encourage your team to find some time for reflection.

As a leader, it is essential to reflect on your own personal strengths and think about how you can honor and exemplify the strengths of your team members. In this chapter, we'll look at how you can use reflection to identify these strengths (and

those of your team members) and to amplify strengths-based conditions, interests, and perspectives.

REFLECT TO IDENTIFY STRENGTHS

Take a moment to reflect on your own strengths and the strengths of your team members. Some strengths may be easy to identify, and others may be harder to determine. Team members may need help recognizing and identifying their strengths, and completing a strength-finding assessment can help. You can find a number of online assessments, such as Clifton Strengths Finder 2.0 (Rath, 2007) from Gallup, which is what our team used, to help you learn more about your strengths and those of your team members. This type of assessment has helped our team identify ways to strengthen our team and our work within the early childhood community. When choosing an assessment tool, make sure to select one that is evidence based and informed by scientific research.

Remember, assessments share only some of your strengths. Everyone has both natural strengths and strengths they have developed over time. For example, one of my natural strengths is having a great desire to learn and continually improve myself. One of my developed strengths is building strong relationships with others. You may find that assessments often highlight your natural strengths rather than your developed strengths, but both are important to your work as a leader.

- Take an online strength assessment to learn more about your natural strengths. Were there any surprises? Reflect on both your natural and developed strengths.
- Invite your team to take an online strength assessment to learn more about their natural strengths. Discuss the findings with your team. Invite team members to reflect on both their natural and developed strengths.

REFLECT ON HOW TO AMPLIFY STRENGTH-BASED CONDITIONS

Once your team members have identified their strengths, you can reflect on how your working environment supports these strengths. Leaders can be instrumental in helping others amplify their best selves; they concentrate on what is working rather than what is not working. For example, it is more productive for a leader to spend time and energy learning about why people are staying in their organization than why people are leaving. As I reflected about what was working well in my organization, I realized that my team members have higher levels of motivation and productivity when I focus on their strengths and amplify strengths-based conditions. Strengths-based conditions include focusing on finding solutions to challenges together, addressing issues respectfully, and giving each other moral support. The unique characteristics, gifts, and contributions of each team member are valued and used to strengthen the team. We also recognized that sometimes we perceive situations differently and need to be open to learning more about how others view the world.

Each of us has a different perception of reality. Our perceptions often fluctuate between strengths-based (focusing on what people are doing right) and deficit-based (focusing on what people are doing wrong) viewpoints. It is important for leaders to reflect on what is working and amplify those aspects. Create conditions that bring out the best in yourself and your team. Let your team members know that they are valued and that they are engaged in meaningful work. Recognize that ideal conditions may vary from person to person. What helps you be your best self?

Personally, I am my best self when I am physically and emotionally healthy. I also find my best self when my work environment is emotionally safe and my interactions with team members are encouraging and respectful. As mentioned earlier, creating an emotionally safe environment takes time and patience. It can help to give team members ongoing opportunities to engage in open communication and reflect together. Remember, mistakes will be made, misunderstandings may occur, and team members may disagree, but strengths-based conditions improve the likelihood that they will be able to resolve these differences. We are each on own journey of development. It may take longer for some team members to feel safe and valued within your team. Be persistent and continue to seek ways to amplify strengths-based conditions.

- Reflect, and then identify the conditions that bring out the best in yourself.
- Ask your team members to reflect and then identify the conditions that bring out their best selves.

Once you and your team identify the optimum conditions, determine how to amplify those conditions. For example, our team has focused on learning more about the types of self-care that promote our physical and emotional health. One of our team members has taught us strategies such as deep-breathing exercises that can help decrease stress. We have taken time during meetings to get to know each other on a more personal level, and that exercise has helped to promote an emotionally safe environment. We have focused on joy and gratitude, which has resulted in our interaction becoming more encouraging and considerate.

Our team is energized when we focus on strengths and what is going well. In contrast, when negativity prevails, team members become defensive and deflated. Focusing on the positive does not mean that you don't address tough issues and topics. You do, but the focus is on finding strengths-based solutions. One way to amplify strength-based conditions is by giving team members opportunities to pursue projects that reflect their interests and strengths, as discussed in more detail in the next section.

FOSTER STRENGTHS-BASED INTERESTS

Leaders can foster team members' strengths-based interests by involving them in projects that match their passions. I invite my team to share ideas—based on their interests—that they think would have a positive effect on early childhood professionals, children, and families. We often brainstorm ideas to determine how different projects could fit into the work we are doing, and it's exciting when one of the ideas really takes off!

> Robin, one of my team members, became interested in makerspaces. A makerspace is a space where children create, problem solve, and explore a variety of materials as they make things either independently or cooperatively with others. I invited Robin to develop a plan for how her interest could be integrated into our work. She researched the concept of makerspaces in early childhood and then presented a plan for how makerspaces could enhance her work. She had well-thought-out ideas, and I encouraged her to move forward with her plan. Additionally, she involved our team in her work, and they began offering makerspace experiences at child-care centers. Makerspace experiences were met with great interest in our community, especially among early childhood professionals who were familiar with *Making It*, a reality competition television show starring Amy Poehler and Nick Offerman.
>
> Teachers and directors involved in makerspace experiences began asking for more resources on the topic. As information on makerspaces for early childhood was rather limited, I approached our team about writing a book and submitted a book proposal to a publisher. Three team members expressed interest and we began writing. Our proposal was accepted. We dubbed our group the "fantastic four" and began working collaboratively on writing. Every two to three weeks we met, reviewed what had been written, suggested revisions, and determined next steps. We worked together, honoring the expertise and strengths of each team member. One person was extremely gifted at writing the stories about our experiences. Another person was good at editing and organizing our work. We divided the work tasks accordingly. One strength of the group was everyone's ability to be open to feedback. It also helped that we kept a consistent, steady pace of output, which prevented feeling overwhelmed about meeting our deadlines. By honoring the strengths of each person—Robin Marx-Mackerley, Sarah Wright, Cathy Peshlakai, and myself—we were able to publish the book *Making Space for Preschool Makerspaces* in 2021.

Fostering strengths-based interests is not limited to your staff or your organizational setting; you can also apply this concept when working with young children. Teachers honor the strengths of the children in their classrooms when they give them opportunities to pursue their interests.

> In Stephanie's classroom, Erik was interested in babies because he had a new baby sister. Stephanie reflected upon Erik's interest and decided to create a unit of study on babies. She added materials to the classroom that included baby dolls, blankets, strollers, car seats, and toys. She invited Erik's mother to bring the baby to class and talk about how they were caring for her. After the visit, the children in Stephanie's classroom became interested in caring for the baby dolls. They took turns feeding them and rocking them to sleep. Erik loved telling his friends stories about his baby sister and what she was learning to do. Stephanie noticed that Erik was taking the lead in initiating play, based on his interest. He was more engaged in his interactions with the other children and was excited to come to school. His mother thanked Stephanie for noticing and acting on Erik's interest. She shared that it had really helped him adjust to having a new baby sister in their home.

Leaders can do many things to foster the strengths-based interests of their team members. The first is to notice their interests. Then, determine how you can create a climate where these interests can be amplified. For example:

- Establish an atmosphere that promotes support for each person's expertise.
- Recognize the strengths of each member of the team, and emphasize those strengths.
- Foster a climate that is respectful and encouraging.
- Give team members ongoing opportunities to develop and share their expertise.

In the final section of this chapter, we will discuss how you and your team can use reflection to change how you perceive situations, which, in turn, can make for a stronger leader and a stronger team.

USE REFLECTION TO GAIN STRENGTHS-BASED PERSPECTIVES

By engaging in ongoing reflection about our values and perspectives, we develop a greater awareness of ourselves and others, which can lead to deeper understanding of our life and leadership. Reflection can give us time to evaluate and process our thoughts and feelings, which can help us understand and gain a strengths-based perspective. Leaders and teams with strengths-based perspectives are more likely to emphasize diversity, inclusion, and equity. They foster courage and resilience. In addition, teachers with strengths-based perspectives come to their classrooms each day with a focus on what is going right versus what is going wrong. They recognize that every child has great potential and growth happens over time. They honor a child's home language and culture. They know that relationships matter and that everyone can contribute when given the right opportunities. To get started, ask yourself the following questions:

- As a leader, do you see abundance or scarcity? For example, when you look at the materials you have in your program, are you grateful for what you have or are you always wishing you had more?
- Are you more likely to encourage or discourage others with your words and actions? More likely to praise others or criticize?
- Are your words and actions given in a spirit of approval or disapproval? Do you generally approve of the work of others, or are you more likely to disapprove of the work of others and find it easier to fix it yourself?
- Are you more likely to invite or mandate participation? Do you give others the option to choose how they will participate, or do you require them to participate in a certain way?
- Is your leadership strengths-based or deficit-based? Do you see and look for what others are doing well or what they are not doing well?
- How connected or disconnected are you with your team members? Do you have close relationships with each of your team members, or is your relationship more distant?
- Are you more solution focused or problem focused when issues arise? What do you focus on first when issues arise? Do you focus on how to solve the issue or on how the problem is causing you concerns you would rather not deal with right now?
- Do you have more of a growth mindset (more adaptive, willing to try new things, and enjoy learning and developing skills and abilities) or a fixed mindset (avoid challenges and feel that abilities can't improve)?

As you ponder these questions, complete the following exercise for yourself as a leader. Then, invite your team to complete the exercise.

RISE AND SHINE PERSPECTIVE EXERCISE

Look at each pair of the following statements. Place an X on each continuum to reflect the perspective that most closely matches your own. For example, if you perceive both abundance and scarcity, place an X in the middle of the continuum. If you perceive abundance more often than scarcity, place an X closer to the word *Abundance.*

Abundance	Scarcity
Encourage	Discourage
Spirit of Approval	Spirit of Criticism
Invite	Mandate
Strengths-based	Deficit-based
Connected	Disconnected
Solution-focused	Problem-focused
Growth Mindset	Fixed Mindset

- What did you find out about yourself?
- Are you comfortable with where you are on the continuum?
- What are your strengths?
- Are there any areas that you could strengthen to become a more joyful leader?

- Invite your team to complete the exercise. What did you discover about your team? What are their strengths and opportunities for growth?

Reflect on what you learned about strengths-based perspectives after completing this exercise. You can enhance the productivity and engagement of your team by focusing on the strengths of each member. The strongest teams are made up of individuals with diverse strengths. Become a joyful, strengths-based leader, reflect on how you can best invest in your team member's strengths, and then watch your team thrive.

DISCUSSION QUESTIONS

1. What does *reflection* mean to you?

2. When and where are you able to engage in your best reflection?

3. What are your natural and developed strengths as a leader?

4. What are the natural and developed strengths of your team members?

5. What conditions bring out the best in you and your team members?

6. What strengths-based interests could you foster in your team members?

____

____

____

7. What did you learn about yourself and your team members after completing the Rise and Shine Perspective Exercise?

____

____

____

REFLECTION ACTIVITY: THREE KEY POINTS

What are three key points you want to remember from your reading?

1. ______________________________
2. ______________________________
3. ______________________________

ACTION PLAN

Determine one or more actions you will take this month to use reflection to build strengths.

- Action:

  ____

  ____

  ____

- Why is this action important?

  ____

  ____

  ____

- What are my next steps?

  ____

  ____

  ____

As a leader, you can have a joyful influence on others. Sometimes your influence as a leader will be known, and sometimes it will be unknown. If just one person is inspired to make positive joyful changes based on something you taught, your influence has made a difference. How much greater will the influence be if two, ten, one hundred, or more people are inspired to make positive joyful changes? They can, in turn, influence and inspire others to make changes.

Finding the joyful leader within is not an event; it is a journey. There will be joy and struggle. You will rise as a leader as you reimagine your purpose, radiate a joyful outlook, engage in joyful actions, create caring connections, and reflect on strengths. Embrace each moment. Rise and shine. Remember, your journey has just begun!

Thank you for joining me in this journey. I would love to hear about your joyful leadership journey. You are invited to email me at teresa@byingtons.net.

Appendices

- Appendix A: **BOOK-CLUB SESSION OUTLINE**
- Appendix B: **JOYFUL SCAVENGER HUNT**
- Appendix C: **JOYFUL BINGO**
- Appendix D: **JOYFUL BEGINNING IDEAS**
- Appendix E: **JOYFUL WELCOME FORM**

APPENDIX A

BOOK-CLUB SESSION OUTLINE

For each book-club session, invite team members to read one or more chapters in this book and complete the discussion questions, reflection activities, and action plan at the end of each chapter.

Invite members to take turns leading the discussion, and start each session with a joyful beginning (see appendix D).

During each book-club meeting, invite members to form small groups and discuss their responses to the reflection activity. Then, bring the group back together and have each small group share a summary of their discussion. Dig deeper into each chapter by talking about responses to the discussion questions. End the book club by giving members time to reflect and connect on how they will apply the information in their practices. (See the sample session and sample outline below for additional information to help you facilitate your book club.)

SAMPLE SESSION

This sample session is timed to last about an hour. Adjust the time to accommodate the needs of your group.

ITEM	GROUPING	TIMING
• Welcome by discussion leader • Joyful beginning by one of the members	Whole group	10 minutes
Discussions on reading reflection activity from the week's chapter	Small groups of 3–5 people	10 minutes
One person from each small group shares a main idea from their discussion	Whole group	5 minutes
Conversation about several of the discussion questions	Small groups of 3–5 people	20 minutes
Discussion of main takeaways	Whole group	10 minutes
Reflect and Connect—Time to reflect on how to apply the information in their practice	Whole group	3 minutes
Closing thoughts by the discussion leader	Whole group	2 minutes

SAMPLE OUTLINE FOR SESSION ON CHAPTER 1: WHY JOY?

ITEM	GROUPING	TIMING
• Welcome by discussion leader • Joyful beginning: Everyone is invited to share three things that bring them joy	Whole group	10 minutes
Discussions on 3-2-1 reading reflection activity: • Three ideas you want to remember • Two things you want to do • One question you would like to discuss	Small groups of 3–5 people	10 minutes
One person from each small group shares a main idea from their discussion such as the following: • Being joyful can improve your life, work, and well-being • Taking time to recognize the joyful moments that naturally occur during the day • Joyspotting	Whole group	5 minutes
Conversation about several of the discussion questions	Small groups of 3–5 people	20 minutes
Discussions on 3-2-1 reading reflection activity: • Three ideas you want to remember • Two things you want to do • One question you would like to discuss	Whole group	10 minutes
Reflect and Connect—Time to reflect on how to apply the information in their practice	Whole group	3 minutes
Closing thoughts by the discussion leader	Whole group	2 minutes

APPENDIX B

JOYFUL SCAVENGER HUNT

Use this activity to add a joyful beginning to your team meeting. One week prior to the meeting, invite everyone to participate in a Joyful Scavenger Hunt. Give each team member this list, and invite them to find different kinds of joyful items and list what they found. At the meeting, ask each team member to share one or more of the items they found.

Joyful Scavenger Hunt

Find something joyful and list what you find.

* In your classroom or office:

  ____

  ____

* Outside in nature:

  ____

  ____

* To eat:

  ____

  ____

* To smell:

  ____

  ____

* To touch:

* To listen to:

* To read:

* In your favorite color:

* To share with someone else:

* You haven't noticed before:

* That makes you smile:

APPENDIX C

JOYFUL BINGO

Cross off the box of each joyful thing that you do during the week. At the end of the week, share with your team members how many joyful things you did.

J	O	Y	F	U	L
Watch a sunset	Stop and smell the flowers	Your choice	Wrap yourself in a soft, warm blanket	Cook a favorite food or try a new recipe	Call a friend
Smile at a stranger	Your choice	Enjoy the blue sky	Share a favorite memory with someone	Dance joyfully	Write in a journal
Wake up without an alarm	Wear something that helps you feel joyful	Set up a display of joyful things	Secretly serve someone you love	Watch the sun rise	Your choice
Savor a favorite food	Go outside and just listen	Share a joyful picture or video	Your choice	Enjoy a favorite hobby	Have a picnic (inside or outside)
Your choice	Light a candle and enjoy the scent	Watch a baby's face for at least 5 minutes	Play a game	Send a note of appreciation	Take a picture of something joyful
Go on a walk and notice the beauties of nature	Doodle or color	Read a book for fun	Take an extra-long warm bath or shower	Your choice	Listen to some beautiful music

Write down what you did for any of the "your choice" squares. How many squares did you complete?

APPENDIX D

JOYFUL BEGINNING IDEAS

The following are ideas for every week of the year. Try some of them, or be creative and think of ways to adapt the ideas for even more joyful beginnings!

* Invite everyone to share something joyful from their week. (This is an exercise that you can do repeatedly.)
* Create a word cloud featuring a topic, such as joyful children's books.
* Play Pictionary and have everyone draw a picture that represents a joyful movie title.
* Ask everyone to share a silver lining from their week.
* Share a funny photo or cartoon, and ask everyone to write a joyful caption.
* Play Name That Tune and have everyone guess the titles of joyful songs.
* Play Two Truths and a Lie. Each person shares three statements about themselves, one of which is not true. Everyone guesses which one is the lie. You can do this over several meetings so that everyone has a chance to share.
* Invite everyone to share a good-news moment from the week.
* Have a dance party! Play a music video and invite everyone to dance along.
* Play a joyful video of children laughing and playing.
* Ask everyone to share a joyful memory from their childhood.
* Invite everyone to share five fun facts about themselves.
* Ask everyone who has a pet to show a picture of their pet and talk about it.
* Invite everyone to create a headline that describes a positive aspect of their week.
* Invite everyone to find a photo on their phone of a joyful place they have visited.
* Invite everyone to wear their joy: find something joyful and describe why it brings joy.
* Share pictures of joyful environments, indoors or out.
* Bring some food for everyone to enjoy.
* Invite everyone to share a favorite joyful quote.

- Post chart paper around the room with questions such as, "What activities do you find joyful?" and "What colors do you find joyful?" Invite everyone to go to each paper and write a response. Highlight similarities and differences.
- Inside-Out: Ask everyone to share something they find joyful inside and outside.
- Invite everyone to write a message to their future self, describing a joyful experience they want to remember.
- Share a story about someone who is spreading joy through their words and actions.
- Sing a joyful song together.
- Food-Fun-Fave: Ask everyone to draw a triangle. In the center write the word *joy*. In one corner, draw a joyful food. In another corner, draw a fun joyful activity. In the third corner, draw a favorite joyful place. Have everyone share their food, fun, and fave.
- Invite everyone to share their favorite season and why they find it joyful.
- Watch a video of a fireworks display. Have everyone describe how they feel when they watch the display.
- Play I Spy. Hide five objects related to your topic before the meeting. Ask everyone to look around the room and find the hidden objects without telling anyone what they found. Then, ask several people to retrieve the objects and bring them up and describe how they relate to the topic being discussed.
- Give everyone a small coloring sheet and some colored pencils. Invite them to enjoy coloring for five minutes and then share their coloring sheet.
- Invite everyone to write a large encouraging message on a blank piece of paper. Then, ask them to walk around the room holding up their paper and silently sharing their message. Ask several people to share a favorite message they saw and why they liked it.
- Play a Unique Trinket Guessing Game. Have someone describe a unique trinket and then have everyone guess what it is. Then, show everyone the trinket.
- Ask everyone to share something joyful they saw this week that they hadn't noticed before.
- Create a PowerPoint presentation featuring something that each person finds joyful.
- Play sounds of ocean waves. Invite everyone to close their eyes and listen to the waves. They can imagine being on a tropical island, enjoying the sandy beach. After a couple of minutes, invite everyone to open their eyes and share what they imagined.
- Invite everyone to write a list of ten things that they are thankful for in their life. Have each person share one to two things from their list.
- Ask everyone to complete the prompt, "I feel joyful when . . ."
- Invite several people to share one of their hidden talents.

- Have Crazy Hair and Happy Hat Day. Invite everyone to come to the meeting with crazy hair or a happy hat.
- Play Guess Who? Collect baby pictures from everyone. Create a slide show and have everyone try to guess who is in each picture.
- Show everyone a picture of a common object, such as a block. Then, give everyone three minutes to write down as many different ways the object could be used as they can. See who can think of the most creative and original responses.
- Go on a short nature walk. Ask everyone to go outside for five minutes and enjoy the beauties of nature. When they return, have them share what they saw and heard.
- Play a matching game. Give everyone a picture card. Use pictures of things that commonly go together, such as peanut butter and jelly. Ask each person to find their match. Talk about how the items can become more joyful when they are combined.
- Play a version of Scattergories. Select four categories such as animals, toys, breakfast foods, and colors. Have someone call out an alphabet letter such as the letter *C*. Then, give everyone about thirty seconds to write a word for each category, such as *coyote, car, cantaloupe,* and *chartreuse*. Continue with three additional letters. Everyone receives one point for each unique answer.
- Invite everyone to share a favorite recipe and tell why the recipe is joyful.
- Invite several people talk about things they collect, and have them describe their collection. If you give them advance notice, they could bring photos or examples from their collection.
- Invite everyone to complete the prompt, "People who are joyful . . ."
- Ask everyone to share the best and most joyful thing that happened to them during past twelve months.
- Invite everyone to share a rose (something that went well), a thorn (something challenging), and a bud (something they are looking forward to in the future).
- Call out different sea creatures and have everyone do corresponding actions such as waving their arms like an octopus and or diving like a dolphin.
- Ask everyone to share where they have traveled or where they would like to go (photos optional).
- In small groups of four to five people, have them identify five things they have in common.
- Find a top ten list, such as top ten qualities of a great early childhood educator, and have small groups try to guess what is on the list. See which group can come up with the most correct responses.

APPENDIX E

JOYFUL WELCOME FORM

We joyfully welcome you to our team! Our team values connections, and we appreciate each person's uniqueness. Please share a few of your favorite joyful things to help us get to know you better.

Name:

Birthday:

Favorite colors:

Snacks, treats, or other foods you enjoy:

Favorite restaurant:

Favorite store to shop:

Favorite sports or sports teams:

Hobbies you enjoy:

Favorite flowers or plants:

Scents you find joyful:

Do you have pets or a favorite animal?

What else do you find joyful?

REFERENCES AND RECOMMENDED READING

Achor, Shawn. 2010. *The Happiness Advantage: How a Positive Brain Fuels Success in Work and Life*. New York: Crown Business.

Alfano, Kathleen. n.d. "10 Ways Adult Can Be More Playful." The Genius of Play. https://thegeniusofplay.org/genius/expert-advice/articles/10-ways-adults-can-be-more-playful.aspx?WebsiteKey=f24671dc-3a61-4dfa-854c-b2d74801f627

Angelou, Maya. 2014. "Be a Rainbow in Someone Else's Cloud." Oprah's Master Class. https://www.youtube.com/watch?v=0nYXFletWH4

Barrett Values Centre. n.d. "Personal Values Assessment." Barrett Values Centre. https://www.valuescentre.com/tools-assessments/pva/

Ben-Shahar, Tal, and Angus Ridgway. 2017. *The Joy of Leadership: How Positive Psychology Can Maximize Your Impact (and Make You Happier) in a Challenging World*. Hoboken, NJ: John Wiley and Sons.

Bishop, Sherri. 2020. "When You Choose Joy." Facebook. https://www.facebook.com/profile/100044402377165/search/?q=when%20you%20choose%20joy

Bliss, Kali. 2020. "How I Optimized My Mind for More Joy and Productivity in Life and Work." Search Engine Journal. https://www.searchenginejournal.com/optimize-mind-joy-productivity-life-work/353626/

Bonebright, Denise A. 2010. "40 Years of Storming: A Historical Review of Tuckman's Model of Small Group Development." *Human Resource Development International* 13(1): 111–120.

Brown, Brené. 2010. *The Gifts of Imperfection*. Minneapolis. MN: Hazelden Publishing.

Brown, Brené. 2013a. "Most of Us Are Afraid and Brave at the Same Moment." Twitter. September 22.

Brown, Brené. 2013b. "The Fast Track to Genuine Joy." Huffington Post. November 27. https://www.huffpost.com/entry/finding-happiness-brene-brown_n_4312653

Brown, Brené. 2018. *Dare to Lead: Brave Work. Tough Conversations. Whole Hearts.* New York: Random House.

Burton, Valorie. 2018. The Most Important Step to Bring Your Vision to Life." Valorie Burton. https://valorieburton.com/the-most-important-step-to-bring-your-vision-to-life/

Burton, Valorie. 2022. “What’s Holding You Back?” Oprah Daily. https://www.oprahdaily.com/life/a40460376/get-unstuck-career-quiz/

Canfield, Jack. 2022. “How to Find Your Purpose in Life.” Jack Canfield (blog). https://jackcanfield.com/blog/how-to-find-your-purpose-in-life/

Chapman, Gary, and Paul White. 2019. *The 5 Languages of Appreciation in the Workplace: Empowering Organizations by Encouraging People*. Chicago, IL: Northfield Publishing.

Cherry, Kendra. 2023. “What Is Toxic Positivity? Verywell Mind. https://www.verywellmind.com/what-is-toxic-positivity-5093958

Chopra, Deepak. 1994. *The Seven Spiritual Laws of Success: A Practical Guide to the Fulfillment of Your Dreams*. San Rafael, CA: Amber-Allen Publishing.

Cohen, Geoffrey L., and David K. Sherman. 2014. “The Psychology of Change: Self-Affirmation and Social Psychological Intervention.” *Annual Review of Psychology* 65: 333–371.

Covey, Stephen M. R. 2018. *The Speed of Trust: The One Thing that Changes Everything*. New York: Free Press.

Covey, Stephen R. 2004. *The 7 Habits of Highly Effective People: Powerful Lessons in Personal Change.* New York: Free Press.

Dahhaj, Zaid. 2018. “Why You Must Name Your Fears to Conquer Them.” Medium. https://zaidkdahhaj.medium.com/why-you-must-name-your-fears-to-conquer-them-7a3810ff0f16

Dahl, Roald. 1980. *The Twits*. London, UK: Jonathan Cape, Ltd.

Dudley, Drew. 2010. “Everyday Leadership.” TEDx Toronto. https://www.ted.com/talks/drew_dudley_everyday_leadership?language=en

Dvorak, Nate, and Natasha Jamal. 2020. “Maintain and Strengthen Your Culture in Times of Disruption.” Gallup. https://www.gallup.com/workplace/307931/maintain-strengthen-culture-times-disruption.aspx

Elliot, Jeffrey, ed. 1989. *Conversations with Maya Angelou*. Jackson, MS: University of Mississippi Press.

Fry, Ronald. 2019. “Leading Positive Change through Appreciative Inquiry.” Online course. Coursera. https://www.coursera.org/learn/appreciative-inquiry

Gordon, Jon. 2017. *The Power of Positive Leadership: How and Why Positive Leaders Transform Teams and Organizations and Change the World*. Hoboken, NJ: John Wiley and Sons.

Gordon, Jon. 2018. *The Power of Positive Teams: Proven Principles and Practices that Make Great Teams Great.* Hoboken, NJ: John Wiley and Sons.

Gordon, Jon. 2021. The Power of Positive Summit. Virtual event. April 21–28. https://www.powerofpositivesummit.com/

Gordon, Jon, and Damon West. 2019. *The Coffee Bean: A Simple Lesson to Create Positive Change*. Hoboken, NJ: John Wiley and Sons.

Gordon, Jon, Dan Britton, and Jimmy Page. 2013. *One Word that Will Change Your Life*. Expanded edition. Hoboken, NJ: John Wiley and Sons.

Gracián, Baltasar. 1992. *The Art of Worldly Wisdom: A Pocket Oracle*. New York: Doubleday.

High 5 Test. 2022. "Relationship Building: Activities, Examples, and How To. High 5 Test. https://high5test.com/relationship-building/

Hittler, John. 2018. "The Genius of Asking 'What If?' Questions." Forbes. https://www.forbes.com/sites/forbescoachescouncil/2018/05/16/the-genius-of-asking-what-if-questions/?sh=1a6b0a8522ef

Houston, Elaine. 2019. "The Importance of Positive Relationships in the Workplace." Positive Psychology. https://positivepsychology.com/positive-relationships-workplace/

Howard, Arianna. 2020. "The & Principle." Arianna Howard. https://www.ariannahoward.com/product/the-principle/

Iruka, Iheoma, Stephanie Curenton, Tonia Durden, and Kerry-Ann Escayg. 2020. *Don't Look Away: Embracing Anti-Bias Classrooms*. Lewisville, NC: Gryphon House.

Jones, Pam, Vicki Holton, and Angela Jowitt. 2021. "6 Common Team Challenges—How to Overcome Them and Grow Your Team." Bytestart. https://www.bytestart.co.uk/tackle-common-team-challenges-develop-team-performance.html

Kanbanize. n.d. "5 Whys: The Ultimate Root Cause Analysis Tool." Kanbanize. https://kanbanize.com/lean-management/improvement/5-whys-analysis-tool

Kegan, Robert, and Lisa L. Lahey. 2016. *An Everyone Culture: Becoming a Deliberately Developmental Organization*. Boston, MA: Harvard Business Review Press.

Lee, Evie. 2021. "Different Leadership Styles." CPD Online College Knowledge Base. https://cpdonline.co.uk/knowledge-base/business/different-leadership-styles/

Lee, Ingrid Fetell. 2022. "Joy Always Comes Back." Instagram. September 13. https://www.instagram.com/p/CidZmwlPW2Q/?hl=en

Lee, Ingrid Fetell. 2018a. *Joyful: The Surprising Power of Ordinary Things to Create Extraordinary Happiness.* New York: Little, Brown Spark.

Lee, Ingrid Fetell. 2018b. "Where Joy Hides and How to Find It." TED Talk. https://www.youtube.com/watch?v=A_u2WFTfbcg

Lee, Ingrid Fetell. 2019a. "Joyspotting 101." The Aesthetics of Joy. https://aestheticsofjoy.com/2019/06/27/joyspotting-101/

Lee, Ingrid Fetell. 2019b. "The Joyspotter's Guide." http://www.aestheticsofjoy.com/wp-content/uploads/2019/06/AoJ-JoyspottersGuide.pdf?ck_subscriber_id=497201037

Linehan, Marsha. 2014. *DBT Skills Training Manual*. 2nd edition. New York: The Guilford Press.

Lorde, Audre. 2007. *Sister Outsider: Essays and Speeches*. Berkeley, CA: Crossing Press.

Mandela, Nelson. 2007. *Long Walk to Freedom: Autobiography of Nelson Mandela*. Braamfontein, South Africa: Nolwazi Educational Publishing.

Marx-Mackerley, Robin, Teresa A. Byington, Sarah Wright, and Cathy Peshlakai. 2021. *Making Space for Preschool Makerspaces*. Lewisville, NC: Gryphon House.

Melkonian, Lois. 2022. "What are Personal Values?" BetterUp. https://www.betterup.com/blog/does-your-work-match-your-personal-values

MindTools. n.d. "5 Whys: Getting to the Root of a Problem Quickly. https://www.mindtools.com/pages/article/newTMC_5W.htm

Mulder, P. 2012. "5 Whys (Root Cause Analysis): Method and Examples." Toolshero. https://www.toolshero.com/problem-solving/5-whys-analysis/

Myers, Vernā. n.d. "How to Overcome Our Biases? Walk Boldly Toward Them." TEDxBeaconStreet. https://www.ted.com/talks/verna_myers_how_to_overcome_our_biases_walk_boldly_toward_them?language=en&subtitle=en

Naiman, Linda. 2021. "What Is Creativity? (And Why Is It a Crucial Factor for Business Success?)" Creativity at Work. https://www.creativityatwork.com/what-is-creativity/

O'Leary, John. 2016. *On Fire: The 7 Choices to Ignite a Radically Inspired Life*. New York: Gallery Books.

Oswald, Andrew J., Eugenio Proto, and Daniel Sgroi. 2015. "Happiness and Productivity." *Journal of Labor Economics* 33(4): 789–822.

Price, Catherine. 2021. *The Power of Fun: How to Feel Alive Again*. New York: The Dial Press.

Rath, Tom. 2007. *StrengthsFinder 2.0. Discover Your Clifton Strengths*. New York: Gallup Press.

re:Work. n.d. "Guide: Understand Team Effectiveness." Re:Work with Google. https://rework.withgoogle.com/guides/understanding-team-effectiveness/steps/introduction/

Ritzi, Evelyn. 2020. "Resilience and Unexpected Joy." LinkedIn. https://www.linkedin.com/pulse/resilience-unexpected-joy-evelyn-ritzi

Rogers, Fred. 1995. *You Are Special: Neighborly Words of Wisdom from Mister Rogers*. New York: Penguin Books.

Rosales, Robert M. 2016. "Energizing Social Interactions at Work: An Exploration of Relationships That Generate Employee and Organizational Thriving." *Open Journal of Social Sciences* 4(9): 29–33.

Ruth, Katrina. 2019. "7 Steps to Living Your Life with Purpose." Entrepreneur. https://www.entrepreneur.com/living/7-steps-to-living-your-life-with-purpose/336600

Scott, S. J. 2019. "What is Your Why? 12 Steps to Find Your Purpose in Life." Develop Good Habits. https://www.developgoodhabits.com/your-why/

Tanner, O. C. 2022. "How Does Leadership Influence Organizational Culture?" O. C. Tanner. https://www.octanner.com/insights/articles/2019/10/23/how_does_leadership_.html

Tenzin, Gyatso. 2001. *The Dalai Lama: The Compassionate Life*. Boston, MA: Wisdom Publications.

Tracy, Brian, n.d. "How to Become an Optimist: 19 Tips to Stay Positive." Brian Tracy International. https://www.briantracy.com/blog/personal-success/be-an-optimist-at-all-times/

Udoagwu, Kelechi. 2021. "How to Build Trust in a Team." Wrike. https://www.wrike.com/blog/how-to-build-trust-in-a-team-at-work/#Why-does-trust-matter-at-work

White, Paul. 2022. "5 Employee Appreciation Languages in the Workplace." Blueboard (blog). https://www.blueboard.com/blog/in-your-own-words-the-5-languages-of-employee-appreciation

Wilson, Carol. n.d. "Bruce Tuckman: The Forming, Storming, Norming and Performing Teach Development Model." Culture at Work. https://www.coachingcultureatwork.com/bruce-tuckman-team-development-model/

Wong, Kellie. 2020. "9 Tips for Building Trust in the Workplace." Achievers. https://www.achievers.com/blog/building-trust-workplace/

Yim, JongEun. 2016. "Therapeutic Benefits of Laughter in Mental Health: A Theoretical Review." *The Tohoku Journal of Experimental Medicine* 239(3): 243–249.

Zak, Paul J. 2017. "The Neuroscience of Trust." Harvard Business Review. https://hbr.org/2017/01/the-neuroscience-of-trust

INDEX

E

F

G

H

I

J